Railways of the Llynfi Valley

RAILWAYS OF THE LLYNFI VALLEY

CLIVE SMITH

ALUN BOOKS
3 Crown Street, Port Talbot, West Glamorgan

ISBN 0 907117 38 4 (casebound)
ISBN 0 907117 39 2 (soft cover)

Printed by Bridgend Printing Co. Ltd., Tremains Road, Bridgend, Mid Glam.

Acknowledgements

My thanks and grateful acknowledgements are due to the following for their help in the preparation of this book:

Mr. E.R. Mountford, Caerphilly, for his kindness in providing information on the locomotives of the Llynfi Valley, together with other additional data, and for reading and correcting my manuscript;

Mr. John Lyons, Mr. Les Buckingham and Mr. J. O'Flynn for sharing their invaluable local knowledge;

Mr. R.L. Pittard, Penyfai, for the use of photographs, for identifying locomotive series and for providing additional data;

Mrs. Julie Jones (Baglan), for the drawings of various maps, plans and track layouts;

The Editor of the Glamorgan Gazette, for allowing me to make reference to the various editions of the newspaper noted in the text;

Miss Susan Thomas (Nantyfyllon) for her undying patience in typing the manuscript;

Mr. Andrew Morris (Nantyfyllon) for drawing the pen-sketch of Pontrhydycyff Viaduct used for the cover illustration;

Mr. A.J. Flint, Caerphilly, and Mr. R.A. Cooke, Oxford, for their very kind assistance;

The County Archivist, County Records Office, Cardiff; Miss Gillian John, Maesteg Library; the librarians at Taibach Reference Library (Port Talbot) and Cardiff Central Reference Library; and the P.R.O.s at B.R. Cardiff and Paddington, for their kind assistance;

Mrs. Lynne Self and Mrs. Anne Jones for photographs and additional information;

The authors of the various publications noted in the text, for allowing me to make reference to their works;

Mr. A. King Davies and Dr. Graham Humphrys for allowing me to make reference to their contributions published in the Souvenir Brochures of the Maesteg District, as noted in the text;

The members of both the Maesteg Historical Society and the Cymmer Afan Historical Society;

The following for providing photographs and other information;

Mrs. Glynis Harvey, Maesteg;
Mr. and Mrs. V. Chilcott, Bettws;
Mr. Walter Wells, Maesteg;
Mr. William Hurd, Bryn;
Mr. Byron Gage, Duffryn Rhondda, Afan Valley;
Mr. James King, Llangynwyd;
Mr. John Morgan, Cymmer;
Mr. D. Maggs, Cymmer;
Mr. Royston M. Davies, Caerau;
Mr. Wyn Jenkins, Maesteg;
Dr. Lynn Jones, Maesteg;

Finally, to my wife and family goes my gratitude for their support and unfailing patience.

Foreword

It seems a natural progression to follow the story of the Afan Valley railways with that of the Llynfi Valley railways. Firstly, both valleys are in very close proximity to each other, and secondly it was the Llynvi and Ogmore Railway Company which linked the two valleys together in 1877 with the construction of the Maesteg tunnel.

In many respects life in both valleys experienced the same pattern, being first agricultural, then industrial, followed by unemployment and decline in recent years. The Llynfi Valley, however, has not suffered as greatly as the Afan Valley.

Again, in the Llynfi Valley, mineral traffic is still carried over the old Great Western line from Nantyfyllon to Tondu junction, whereas all railtracks in the Afan Valley were removed in 1971.

I travelled many times from Cymmer General Station in the Afan Valley to Maesteg Castle Street in the Llynfi Valley and have very fond memories of that journey. Thus it is hoped that for many readers this book will enable them to recall the happy times they experienced travelling on the lines of the Llynfi Valley railways. For others, it is hoped that they will find the ensuing pages informative and of interest.

CLIVE SMITH.

April 1984.

The armorial device of the Duffryn Llynvi and Porthcawl Railway.
(By Courtesy of Mr. A. J. Flint and the Kenfig Hill and District Music and Arts Society).

Contents

Illustrations

Frontispiece: The armorial device of the Duffryn Llynvi and Porthcawl Railway. (By courtesy of Mr. A.J. Flint and the Kenfig Hill and District Music and Arts Society.)

Map showing the routes of the railways in the Llynfi Valley.

Map of the Duffryn Llynvi and Porthcawl Railway. (By permission of the Kenfig Hill Music and Arts Society.)

Track layouts of the Upper Llynfi Valley: redrawn from original copies. (By courtesy of R.A. Cooke.)

Plan of the Llynvi Iron Works, Maesteg, 1876. (By courtesy of Dr. Graham Humphrys, Geography Department, Swansea University College.)

Plan of the proposed Ogmore Dock and Railway, 1883. (By courtesy of the Editor of the Glamorgan Gazette.)

Sunday Excursion Advertisements, Glamorgan Advertiser, August 13th 1948.

    a) Maesteg Castle Street to Porthcawl, Summer 1948.
    b) Abergwynfi to Porthcawl, Summer 1948.

Copy of Announcements of Football Excursions to Ninian Park, 1960-1961.

Advertisement, Glamorgan Advertiser, August 13th, 1948, of Maesteg Chamber of Trade annual outing to Bath.

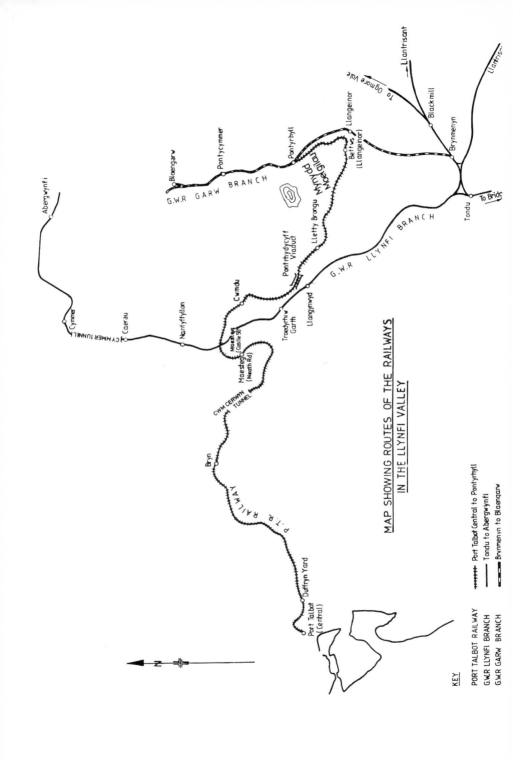

MAP SHOWING ROUTES OF THE RAILWAYS
IN THE LLYNFI VALLEY

KEY

┿┿┿┿┿┿ Port Talbot Central to Pontyrhyll
──────── Tondu to Abergwynfi
▅▅▅▅▅ Brynmenyn to Blaengarw

PORT TALBOT RAILWAY
G.W.R LLYNFI BRANCH
G.W.R GARW BRANCH

Abergwynfi

Cymmer
CYMMER TUNNEL
Caerau
Nantyffyllon
Maesteg (Castle St)
Maesteg (Neath Rd)
CWM CERWYN TUNNEL
Bryn
P.T.R RAILWAY
Duffryn Yard
Port Talbot (Central)

Blaengarw
Pontycymmer
G.W.R GARW BRANCH
Pontyrhyll
Mynydd Morgraig
Bettws (Llangeinor)
Llangeinor
To Ogmore Vale
Llantrisant
Llantrisant
Blackmill
Brynmenyn
Tondu
To Bridg

Cwmdu
Lletty Brongu
Pontrhydycyff Viaduct
Troedyrhiw Garth
Llangynwyd
G.W.R LLYNFI BRANCH

N

Introduction

Early Industrial History of the Llynfi Valley.

The Llynfi Valley runs north to south, with Margam Mountain and the South Wales coastline to the west and the Garw and Ogmore Valleys to the east. It is the largest and easiest of the natural approaches of the three parallel valleys (Llynfi, Garw and Ogmore), which converge on Tondu. There the river Llynfi meets the Ogmore river approximately four miles from Bridgend. The river Ogmore flows through Bridgend and is joined by the waters of the Ewenny just south of the Priory, to enter the Severn Estuary at Ogmore-by-Sea.

Returning up the valley from Tondu, the Llynfi Valley gradually closes within high hills, but after about five miles, tending to the north-west, it opens out at Maesteg into one of the widest of the Mid-Glamorgan valleys. Three miles further on it enters into a cul-de-sac of mountains, and here, in Mynydd-y-Caerau (1823 ft.), the Llynfi river has its several sources, the chief being at Coedcae-ffyrch. Mynydd-y-Caerau separates the Llynfi Valley from the Afan Valley.

The upper course of the Llynfi is enveloped by mountains: Y Foel Fawr (1147 ft.), Foel-y-Dyffryn (1202 ft.), Y Garnwen (1182 ft.) and Y Mynydd Bach (Pwll-yr-Iwrch, 1421 ft.)[1]

Caerau is the northernmost township in the Llynfi Valley. Below Caerau, and adjoining, are Nantyfyllon, Maesteg (the main town), Garth, Cwmfelin, Pontrhydycyff (Llangynwyd), Coytrahen and Tondu. The whole length of the valley is some six to seven miles.

The Llynfi Valley, which once formed part of the ancient district of Tir Iarll[2], was, in the eighteenth century, a landscape of scattered white-washed farms, with the village of Llangynwyd and its ancient parish church perched on the hill top. The district in those days was a most attractive area, a picturesque valley of singular charm, honoured by the bards of Morgannwg (Glamorgan).

Apart from stock-raising on the hilly slopes, the farms produced sufficient food to meet the needs of the local inhabitants. Corn was ground at the mills in the area, namely Melin Maesteg and Melin Pontrhydycyff, while spinning of wool was carried out in the homes of the people as well as in the spinning mills at Cwmfelin and Gadlys. It was an altogether peaceful, pastoral scene.

The local farmers depended entirely on what they produced, but the mountains never gave back the true value of the work that was put into them. However most of these small farms benefitted from the seams of coal that were found on the mountain side, and which initially the farmers mined for their own domestic use, until, realising the value of this mineral, they commenced mining on a commercial basis. Henry John, in his paper on the Iron Industry in Maesteg in the nineteenth century, states 'Records of sales of coal to customers in the Vale of Glamorgan indicated a considerable traffic. This was borne out by the numerous 'holloways' found on the slopes of the mountains leading down into the valley. They are marked on early O.S. maps as entrenchments but are, in fact, tracks worn by pack mules. The direction, and heavy wear of some of them, indicate something more than the commerce of farming.'

During the second half of the eighteenth century coke had superseded charcoal as the fuel used in iron making. The abundance of coking coal and iron ore found locally and the availability of limestone in outlying districts resulted in the development of iron making in the Maesteg district in the early nineteenth century, with local farmers selling or leasing their land to enterprising landlords and profit-seeking ironmasters.

Thus it was that in May 1826 the Maesteg Iron Company was floated (the Old Works), in the vicinity of South Parade. Furnaces were constructed from local stone. Brickworks were erected to make bricks from local clay for the ovens and two coal levels were opened out, providing employment for large numbers of men.[5]

As a result of this early industrial activity a constant influx of workers came to the area. The Maesteg Iron Company built houses for its workers at Garnlwyd, South Parade and Company

2

Row, while managers had mansions (such as Plasnewydd) built for them.[5]

In 1831 James Allen established the 'Spelter Works' near the Coegnant stream at Caerau. Until that date this district was known as Duffryn Llynfi, but it became known as 'Spelters' with the opening of the new industry of spelting at that place. Then, later, at the turn of the century, a change of name came about once more, and 'Spelters' was replaced by Caerau. It was from this region of the Llynfi Valley that a horse-drawn tramway ran to Porthcawl. At the outset, in 1828, the tramway connected the Maesteg Ironworks to the port at Porthcawl, but later, c. 1831, it was connected to the 'Spelter Works' (situated north of the Maesteg Ironworks) via the initial terminus at Garnlwyd.[8] Porthcawl was the principal port for the district in those days of development, and to some extent grew to industrial importance alongside that of Maesteg.

In 1839 James Allen and partners established another iron company, the Cambrian Iron Works (later known as the Llynvi Iron Works),[8] on the site where the new Sport Centre is situated today. In 1846 the 'Forge' was added to these works.

Prior to 1861 coal mined locally was used mainly to supply the iron works in the Maesteg district, while iron was hauled from the 'Old Patch'[3] workings to the furnaces, and then from the furnaces was taken by tramroad. By 1861 the horse-drawn tramway had been superseded by steam traction on a new railway system in the valley. The advent of the steam railway opened up new markets for coal, resulting in larger levels being dug and deeper collieries being sunk. In 1863 the No. 9 level (near Brynrhug) was opened. Garth Pit was sunk in 1865 and Oakwood Colliery in 1868.[4]

In the meantime the population of the valley had grown rapidly and many workers had arrived in the region to seek work in the coal mines, from near and far, from districts in West Wales, from North Wales, from Cornwall, Somerset and from Ireland -though from the latter they came more especially to work on the construction of the railways. The Irish workmen employed on the construction of the railways were known as 'Navvies', and it is said that at one period there were more than 16 common lodging houses in the Maesteg district accommodating them.

In 1801 the total population of Llangynwyd Upper and Cwmdu hamlets numbered 806, the majority being employed in agricultural occupations, but by 1831 the total population had almost doubled and there was a great increase in the numbers employed in industry. By 1881 the district had changed from a peaceful and picturesque farming valley to a very industrialised region with a population of 8,316.

At this period (c. 1880) the iron industry in the Maesteg district had fallen on hard times and was running down. The Garth Ironworks had closed in the early eighteen fifties and the Maesteg Ironworks (the Old Works) closed in 1873. However, by 1881 coal had become an important commodity in its own right, and there were at that time fourteen collieries[4] working in the valley, in addition to a number of small levels worked on the surrounding mountain sides. The Llynvi Iron Works and the Llwydarth Tin Plate Works were still operating, but the ironworks was experiencing financial constraint and it finally closed in 1886. The Llwydarth Tin Plate works ultimately closed in 1897.

In 1889 a syndicate led by Colonel North (North's Navigation Collieries Ltd.) took over all the assets and mineral rights of the reconstructed Llynvi and Tondu Coal and Iron Company Ltd., for a quarter of a million pounds, and concentrated exclusively on coal mining. Deeper and larger pits were sunk in the Upper Llynfi Valley to reach the richer seams of steam coal at the lower levels.

By the turn of the century the Llynfi Valley had become a flourishing mining district. Thousands of workmen had crowded into the valley; large settlements rose rapidly near their place of work and the established railway communications gave ready access to all the main towns and villages of the region.

Note 1. Ordnance Survey datum 6″ to the mile.
Note 2. The Llynfi Valley was part of the ancient district of 'Tir Iarll' (the Earl's Land), which included the parishes of Llangynwyd, Bettws, Kenfig and Margam in Glamorgan. The name 'Tir Iarll' dates from the time when this portion of Glamorgan came into the possession of Robert Fitzhamon, Earl of Gloucester, in the eleventh century, as a result of the Norman conquest of the county. (TIR IARLL - F. Evans, 1912.)
Note 3. 'Patches' were areas of land where there were outcrops of a mixture of coal and iron-ore known in the district as 'Black Band'. The iron was separated by a process known as roasting, carried out close to the patch site.
Note 4. Dr. Graham Humphrys - The Industrial History of Maesteg. Maesteg Town Hall Centenary Brochure, 1982.
Note 5. D. Davies -Tŷ'r Llwyni. Port Talbot, 1961.
Note 6. B. Richards - History of the Llynfi Valley. D. Brown & Sons, 1982.

Note 7. Extract taken from the Cambrian Newspaper for 10th January 1829.

Advertisement to 'Ironmasters'.

Superior veins of iron and coal to be let on 376 acres on eastern side and 276 acres on western side of River Llynfi. At a moderate royalty for a long term of years.

Note 8. Extract taken from Cambrian Newspaper, 10th January, 1829.

Advertisement to 'Ironmasters'.

Wanted by the Duffryn Llynvi and Porthcawl Rail Road Company, a sufficient quantity of bright grey iron rails (of the same pattern as have already been used, each rail to be three feet ten inches long, and not exceeding 56 lbs in weight), to complete the upper part of the railroad; being a distance of nearly 2¼ miles and requiring about 150 tons - The whole to be delivered at Garn Llwyd where the road at present terminates and which is about 15¼ miles from Porthcawl . . .

GENERAL SOURCES:

F. Evans - Tir Iarll. Cardiff, 1912.

H. John - The iron industry of Maesteg in the nineteenth century: An outline. *In* The Journal of the S.E. Wales Archaeological Society, Vol. 2, No. 2, 1976.

D. Davies - Tŷ'r Llwyni. Port Talbot, 1961.

B. Richards - History of the Llynfi Valley. D. Brown & Sons, Cowbridge, 1982.

Dr. G. Humphrys - The industrial history of Maesteg. Maesteg Town Hall Centenary Brochure, 1982.

Census Reports, 1801, 1831, 1881. Registrar General's Office.

Thomas Bevan - Dissertation on the industrial development of the Llynfi, Ogmore and Garw Valleys, with special reference to transport facilities in the area. Unpublished M.A. Thesis, University of Wales, Cardiff, 1928.

1. The Duffryn Llynvi and Porthcawl Railway (1825-1860)

The roadways of the Llynfi Valley in the early decades of the nineteenth century were completely inadequate for industrial development, being of a dirt track nature in the summer months and quite impassable at times in winter because of mud. The main road of the valley in those days came from the direction of Llantrisant, running via the 'Cerdin' (Cross Inn), up the hill past the 'Red Cow Inn', past Brynmawr Farm to an inn called 'Mount Pleasant' (a wayside inn which was situated on land adjacent to the present Maesteg Golf Clubhouse), and thence to Bryn. It then ran past Penhydd Farm, avoiding Cwmavon, through Pontrhydyfen via Cimla to Neath.[1]

With the development of the coal and iron industries in the upper Llynfi Valley, in the districts of Caerau, Nantyfyllon and Maesteg, there came a need to provide an export outlet to the sea, and so on the 10th June 1825 a company promoted by local landowners and industrialists procured an Act of Parliament to construct a horse-drawn tramway from the upper region of the Llynfi Valley to a harbour at Porthcawl. This tramway was known as the 'Duffryn Llynvi and Porthcawl Railway'.

The Act was decreed 'for making and maintaining a railway or tramway from, or from near to, a certain place called Duffryn Llynfi, in the Parish of Llangonoyd in the county of Glamorgan, to, or near to, a certain Bay called Pwll-y-Cawl in the Parish of Newton Nottage in the same county, and for extending and improving the same Bay, by the erection of a pier and other suitable works for that purpose.'[3]

H.J. Randall mentions in his book, 'Bridgend - a Market Town', that on 26th November 1814 a meeting was held at the

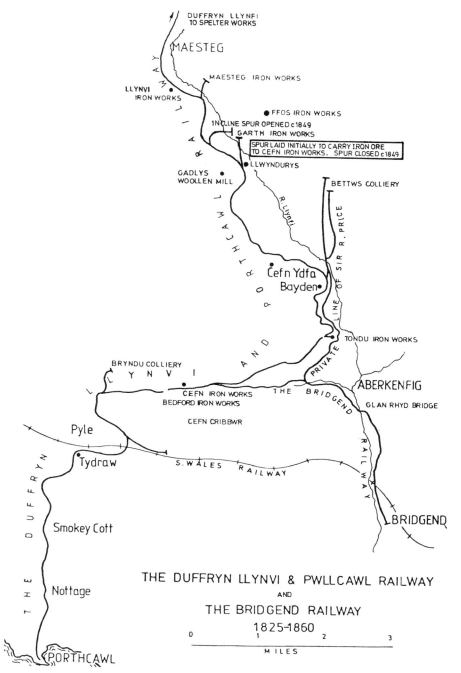

DUFFRYN LLYNFI
TO SPELTER WORKS

MAESTEG

MAESTEG IRON WORKS

LLYNVI
IRON WORKS

● FFOS IRON WORKS

INCLINE SPUR OPENED c1849
GARTH IRON WORKS

SPUR LAID INITIALLY TO CARRY IRON ORE
TO CEFN IRON WORKS. SPUR CLOSED c1849

● LLWYNDURYS

GADLYS ●
WOOLLEN MILL

BETTWS COLLIERY

R. Llynfi

Cefn Ydfa
Bayden ●

TONDU IRON WORKS

BRYNDU COLLIERY
Y N V I

CEFN IRON WORKS
BEDFORD IRON WORKS

THE   BRIDGEND

ABERKENFIG

GLAN RHYD BRIDGE

CEFN CRIBBWR

Pyle

● Tydraw

S. WALES   RAILWAY

BRIDGEND

Smokey Cott

Nottage

THE DUFFRYN LLYNVI & PWLLCAWL RAILWAY

AND

THE BRIDGEND RAILWAY

1825–1860

0   1   2   3

MILES

PORTHCAWL

By permission of the Kenfig Hill Music and Arts Society

7

Wyndham Arms, Bridgend, to consider the laying down of a tramway from Ewenny Bridge northward, up the Llynfi Valley to Duffryn Llynfi[2], with a branch line to Tregunter in the Cefn district and another to Taibach. However, this proposal came to nothing as the suggested route made no connection with the sea, which was essential for any future development of the Llynfi Valley and also the Bridgend district.

In 1818[5] an alternative route was suggested to connect Duffryn Llynfi with the mouth of the Ogmore River. This proposal came under strong objection from Sir John Nicholl, M.P. for Merthyr Mawr, who contended it would adversely affect his property[4], and thus, as already stated, it was the Porthcawl scheme that was finally commissioned in 1825.

Construction of the D.L. & P.R. began in 1826, and the line from Garnlwyd to Porthcawl was opened on 22nd June 1828. The engineer of the line was John Hodgkinson from Newport, Gwent, and as the tramway was worked by horses, which required few gradients, if any, he did a remarkable job in constructing this tramway, for it ran from the mountainous region of the upper Llynfi Valley to the sea at Porthcawl, and only reached the 400 ft. contour in a distance of 18 miles.[5] It had a 4'6" gauge, with iron plates fixed on blocks of holed stones, and fish-bellied iron rails 3' or 3'10" long.

The construction of the Maesteg Iron Works (the Old Works) in 1826 called for the laying down of a tramway to connect with the D.L. & P.R. terminus at Garnlwyd. To make this possible two bridges needed to be constructed, one over Castle Street and the other over the River Llynfi at Bridge Street. The bridge over Castle Street was demolished in 1952 and the keystone, which bears the inscription M.I.C. 1827, is now permanently fixed in the retaining wall at the junction of Castle Street and Bridge Street. The second bridge, crossing the River Llynfi at Bridge Street, still remains, though it has been partly reconstructed to incorporate it in the road-widening scheme undertaken there.

The eventual terminus in c. 1829/30 of the D.L. & P.R. was situated near the present Caerau Square where the old ambulance station stood, with a parting leading over the River Llynfi to the Blaenllynfi Colliery. The tramway proceeded south along the east bank of the River Llynfi to Nantyfyllon (known as Tywith), from whence it crossed the river and continued along Bangor Terrace,

8

behind High Street, crossing the road near the Traveller's Rest Hotel, through the site of the old Llynvi Iron Works to Llynfi Road. It then continued through Commercial Street to Bethania Street and along Llwydarth Road to the Cerdin (Cross Inn); thence to the Llwyndurys weighing house at Pontrhydycyff (Llangynwyd), after which it ran across the main road, and continued behind Maesteg Comprehensive School to the old Gadlys Woollen Mill, where its embankment can be traced across Nant-y-Gadlys. The tramway then continued to Cefn Ydfa and to Tondu, where it turned west to Cefn Cwsc, Kenfig Hill, Pyle, Cornelly and finally to the harbour at Porthcawl.

Llwydarth Road to the Cross Inn at that time was a rough track which forded the stream at Cwm Cerdin, and it was the construction of the tramway which accounted for the bank over the stream being formed. The route of the tramway from Commercial Street to the Cross Inn later became the main road from the Maesteg town centre.[1]

It is often asked how Commercial Street came to be so wide, and the reason for this is given by Mr. A. King Davies (Clerk to the Maesteg Urban District Council 1923-1953): 'When the tramway ran that way, the roadway was only a narrow track. Later, when shops were opened on the river side of this track in what were originally cottages, they were well below the level of the road. Subsequently, when these shops were raised to the level of the street, the line or frontages of the original cottages had to be kept and basements and cellars were created with each shop that was erected. On the other side of the street the boundary walls of the gardens to the cottages became the line of frontage of the new shops.' (At the time of the D.L. & P.R., Commercial Street, Maesteg, was known as Bowrington Street, in respecct to Sir John Bowring, and Bethania Street was then known as Garnlwyd.)

Apart from carrying coal and iron from the Maesteg district to Porthcawl harbour, the D.L. & P.R. carried limestone from the Cornelly district to be used as a flux in the smelting of iron ore. It also carried the zinc ore (spelter) which was brought to Porthcawl in ships from Cornwall, to the 'Spelter Works' at Coegnant for smelting. The zinc was then taken back to Porthcawl for shipment to various parts.

Horses were in general use in the iron works as well as on the tramroad, and initially almost every farm in the area had one

9

horse or more hired out for use in these concerns. In later years, however, the owners of the Iron Works and the tramroad kept their own horses and paid special hauliers. As lime was needed for the smelting of iron, farmers were quick to seize the opportunity to have limestone brought nearer to their farms where kilns were built for the burning of lime, at convenient places along the route.[6]

A regular time table was operated on the line. It usually took a little over six hours to travel from Coegnant to Porthcawl, whilst the return journey took eight hours. At certain places and at stations there was a double track where the trains were able to pass one another. Each train was pulled by a team of three horses.[3]

It is said that when teamsters met between passing places the precedence was often decided by the boy assistants of each team having to fight it out for the right of way, and it is claimed that an area renowned for the practice was Pant y Clotsien (the hollow of the blow) which is situated close to the line of the tramway at the rear of the present Green Meadow houses at Lower Llangynwyd.

The trams were owned by the works and individuals, not by the D.L. & P.R. company.

There was no provision for passenger traffic on the line, but anyone who could afford it could use his own private horse and tram and run it on the line for his own use, provided he paid the required tolls and conformed with the Company regulations, one of which gave precedence to official trains, while another forbade hauliers to ride on the trams. However, the roadway alongside the line was allowed for public use.

The Cambrian Newspaper for 31st December 1841 gave the following account of a fatal accident that occurred to a woman passenger travelling on the tramway.

MAESTEG. On the 24th inst., a fatal accident happened here. A young respectable woman of Thomas Howel of Newtown, Nottage, had left her home for the purpose of spending Christmas day with her relations in Maesteg. She went by a train of trams and, having arrived at her journey's end, she incautiously attempted to get out while the train was proceeding. Her dress caught in the upper part of the tram, she fell between the wheels and was crushed in a pitiful manner.

Assistance was promptly rendered, and she survived but a short time.

Inquest before Thos. Thomas, Esq., Coroner. Accidental death recorded.

There were weighing houses situated at various points along the line where the required rates of toll were displayed; also gates were placed at many points with notices of penalties for failure to keep them closed. The weighing houses were situated at Llwyndurys, Aberkenfig, Ffos, Tydraw and Smokey Cott. The Llwyndurys weighing house was connected initially by a spur to the Garth Iron Works when the works was opened in 1847.[6] Later this works was connected directly to the D.L. & P.R. line. The Llwyndurys weigh-house was known locally as Pwys Dŷ (the Welsh equivalent of weigh-house), but today it is No. 1 Station Road, Llangynwyd, the property of Mr. and Mrs. J. King.

Policemen were employed by the Company to patrol the line to ensure that rules and regulations were adhered to. The Cambrian Newspaper for July 21st 1848 reported a fatal accident that occurred on the line to one unfortunate policeman employed by the Company. The account is as follows: *'Policeman William Rees-Bach, Dyffryn Llynvi-Porthcawl Railway. Killed by horse moving tram. Fell under wheels of tram at Tydraw, Pyle.'*

Besides the stations and weighing houses along the route, there were various buildings and outhouses which contained stables called 'Halts'. It was at these points that horses were changed. Again, men employed as lengthmen were responsible for the maintenance of certain lengths of track along the line. These lengthmen, together with their families, were housed in cottages situated at regular intervals at the side of the tramway.

Under an Act of 1828 a branch line was opened on Friday, October 22nd 1830, from Bridgend (on a site near the present Bridgend bus station) through Aberkenfig to join the D.L. & P.R. at Cwm Ffos in the Cefn district. This horse-drawn track was called the 'Bridgend Railway' and was a separate company from the D.L. & P.R. The engineer of the line was again John Hodgkinson of Newport, Gwent. The Cambrian Newspaper gave the following report of its official opening:

'Bridgend Railway'

'On Friday, October 22, the Bridgend Railway was opened to the public, and though the day proved very wet and unfavourable, a great concourse of persons assembled on the occasion. Twenty tons of coal were brought down from the 'Tyr Gunter Collieries', and distributed among the poor of the town at the expense of the company. The bells of the churches were rung, and cannons continued firing throughout the day.'

In 1835/36 Sir Robert Price, a major shareholder in the Company, leased land and built Tondu Iron Works. He then

11

constructed a private tramway to carry coal from his Bettws Colliery to his iron works and brick works at Tondu where it connected with the D.L. & P.R. at Cwm Ffos.

For over thirty years the D.L. & P.R. served the needs of the Llynfi Valley, which had been virtually cut off from the outside world prior to 1828.

In 1846 construction began on the main South Wales line, and the Bridgend station was opened on 18th June 1850. The D.L. & P.R. was taken over in 1847 by the Llynvi Valley Railway Company, which had been incorporated in 1846, but no progress was made in the construction of a proposed steam railway until an Act was finally obtained in 1855 authorising a broad gauge railway from Bridgend to Tywith.

The reason for much of the delay in securing government sanction to construct a steam railway between these years is attributed to 'prohibitive clauses' being continually put forward by local landowners, which objected to 'the steam engine, with its smoke and noise from entering the town of Porthcawl.' This eventually accounted for a tunnel being built to avoid Nottage Court, on the outskirts of Porthcawl town.[3] Another contributory factor for the delay can be seen in the depressed state of the iron industry at that time.

By 1854 the Bridgend Railway had been incorporated in the L.V.R. Company and construction on the new railway began in July 1858.

(N.B. In his book 'The History of the Llynfi Valley' Mr. Brinley Richards informs us that: 'An exhibition catalogue prepared by the Kenfig Hill and District Music and Arts Society together with all papers, maps and photographs that resulted from the researches of the society led by Mr. Arthur J. Flint and Mr. Bryn James in 1968, have been handed to the National Maritime and Industrial Museum of Wales.')

Note 1. A.K. Davies - Maesteg Town Hall Centenary Brochure, 1981.
Note 2. Duffryn Llynfi is now Maesteg District.
Note 3. Thomas Bevan M.A. - A dissertation on the industrial development of the Llynfi, Ogmore and Garw Valleys. Bridgend, 1928.
Note 4. B. Richards - History of the Llynfi Valley. D. Brown & Sons, Cowbridge, 1982.
Note 5. H.J. Randall - Bridgend - a Market Town. R.H.Johns, Newport, 1955.
Note 6. Thomas Evans - Agricultural and farm notes. Souvenir Brochure, Maesteg, 1958.

SOURCES OF INFORMATION:

A. King Davies - Railways of the Llynfi Valley. Maesteg and District Souvenir Brochure, 1981.

D. Davies - 'Tŷ'r Llwyni'. Port Talbot, 1961.

A. King Davies - Local Government and Civic Affairs. Maesteg Town Hall Centenary Brochure, 1958.

Brinley Richards - History of the Llynfi Valley. D. Brown & Sons, Cowbridge, 1982.

Thomas Bevan M.A. - A dissertaion on the industrial development of the Llynfi, Ogmore and Garw Valleys, with special reference to transport facilities in the area. Bridgend, 1928.

Thomas Bevan M.A. - Mid-Glamorgan Railways. Glamorgan Gazette, 1st July 1966.

H.J. Randall - Bridgend - the story of a Market Town. R.H. Johns, Newport, 1955.

A.J. Flint - The Duffryn Llynvi and Porthcawl Railway 1825-1860. In Morgannwg, Vol. XIII. Glamorgan Historical Society, 1969.

E.T. MacDermot - The history of the Great Western Railway. Vol. 2, 1863-1921. London, 1927. (Revised C.R. Clinker, 1964.

Thomas Evans - Agricultural and farm notes. Souvenir Brochure, Maesteg, 1958.

1841 Tithe Map of the Llynfi Valley. County Records Office, Cardiff.

2. The Llynvi Valley Railway

The Bill of 1855 commissioned the construction of a broad gauge railway line from Tywith to a junction with the main South Wales Railway at Bridgend.[1] Isambard Kingdom Brunel was the engineer appointed to prepare the plans and Mr. Rhind was appointed superintendent.

The first sod for the line was cut on Thursday, 15th July 1858.[1] The official opening was reported in the July edition of 'The Illustrated London News', and the report read as follows:

LLYNFI VALLEY

Turning the First Turf for a Railway.

The Llynfi Valley which is second to none of the Glamorgan Valleys in mineral wealth has hitherto been but partially developed, because its only means of transport has been a tramway winding along the hillsides, and worked very expensively by horses. It is now to have the great advantage of a broad gauge locomotive railway on a low level in connection with the adjacent valleys of Garw and Ogmore and the South Wales line, and consequently with all ports of the Bristol Channel.

The Llynvi Valley Railway was 11 miles long with a 7ft gauge to correspond with the G.W.R. The contractor for the railway was Alexander Brogden, the eldest surviving son of a celebrated family of industrial pioneers of Mid-Glamorgan, John Brogden and Sons. The three eldest sons, John, Alexander and Henry, were expert and experienced railway engineers and had helped to construct the Ulverston and Lancaster Railway in the early 1850s.[2] The construction of the L.V.R. line took three years to complete, and it opened for mineral traffic on the 10th August 1861. Broad gauge rails were laid on the old line from Tondu to Porthcawl about the same time.

14

The L.V.R. did not follow the route of the old Bridgend tramway. Its initial terminus was placed at the goods yard in Coity Road[5]; then, five years later, in 1866, it crossed the bridge and ran into Bridgend Station, where it had its own platform and booking office. This station was approached by a lane behind the Coity Castle Hotel. The old Bridgend tramway became derelict, and was later converted into a public roadway.

The L.V.R. ran from Bridgend Station direct to a new junction at Tondu, from whence it proceeded northward to its terminus at Tywith.[3]

The first official passenger train travelled from Bridgend to Maesteg on 25th February 1864, but it was not until 1st August 1865 that the line from Maesteg to Porthcawl was officially opened for passenger traffic.

Initially the L.V.R. used locomotives and stock supplied by the G.W.R. until two new broad gauge engines were delivered to the Company on the 4th April 1862.[6]

The first station at Maesteg was a single platform adjacent to the old goods shed, with Mr. William Akehurts[7] as its first station master. Later Llangonoyd (Llangynwyd) Station was built, and this platform can still be seen today beyond the road bridge just below the old Llangynwyd G.W.R. Station.

In his thesis, Thomas Bevan remarks that at the same time as the L.V.R. was opened for mineral traffic from Tywith to Bridgend in 1861, J. Brogden & Sons had acquired permission from Parliament to open a broad gauge single railway line 2¼ miles in length from a junction at Tondu to the Cefn District, to connect with the iron and coal industries there.

He then continues by stating that both of these railways had a detrimental effect on the future of the harbour at Porthcawl, for they diverted much of the traffic eastwards to the port of Cardiff, which resulted in a big fall-off in shipments. This prevented the harbour at Porthcawl from becoming a first class Bristol Channel port at that time.

Meanwhile, the arrival of the new steam railway in the upper Llynfi Valley occasioned the laying down of railway lines and tramways to connect with the coal mines and iron works in the district. For the first few weeks of steam raising broad gauge lines operated outside the tramlines, and locomotives worked in conjunction with the horse-drawn tramway on the section between Tondu and Porthcawl. The horse-drawn tramway system very soon became abandoned in the upper Llynfi Valley and the track was converted into roadways.

At this time a bridge was constructed to cross the River Llynfi and the main road at a point near the Colliers Arms, Nantyfyllon. This bridge[4] carried a siding connecting line from the L.V.R. at Llynfi Junction to the Llynvi Iron Works. (The bridge was demolished in 1957 - one abutment remains on the east side of the river.)

It is interesting to note that the South Wales Mineral Railway had designs on extending a line, from its terminal at Glyncorrwg in the Afan Valley, through the Cymmer mountain to Blaenllynfi at the head of the Llynfi Valley, to connect with the iron works in the area. However, this proposal was not sanctioned by Parliament, and as a consequence was not included in the S.W.M.R. Act of 1853.

Again, there were proposal plans drawn up for the construction of a railway line from Aberafan to Cymmer in 1864-65, the railway to be known as the Afon Valley Railway. From these plans it is to be seen that it was the intention of the company to connect the Afan Valley with the Llynfi Valley by the construction of a tunnel through the mountain at Cymmer, to enter the Llynfi Valley near the Llynfi Arms at Blaen Caerau. Though Mr. Gordon McKenzie was appointed its engineer, the proposals came to nothing and it was the later Llynvi and Ogmore Railway Company which eventually joined together the two valleys.

The Advantages of Steam

There is a very interesting song of about 60 verses extant, of the advantages of steam communication between Bridgend and Maesteg, which commenced about the year 1863.

    The company has put on a van,
    Which has succeeded since it began.
    The public say it is a good plan
    To carry passengers all they can,
    Each boy, girl, woman and man,
    By coke and cinders, water and steam,
    Which makes fire to flash and sparks to gleam,
    On the Llynfi Railway.

(From a newspaper cutting in the collection of Cadrawd - T.C. Evans, Llangynwyd, 1846-1918 - 2330 MS59; with acknowledgements to Cardiff Central Library.)

Note 1. Thomas Bevan M.A. - Dissertation, 1928.
Note 2. L.S. Higgins - John Brogden & Sons. *In* The Glamorgan Historian, Vol. 10, Stewart Williams, 1974.
Note 3. 1876 Ordnance Survey datum, 6″ to the mile.
Note 4. 1/9/1859 - Private siding agreement between the L.V.R. and the Llynvi Vale Iron Company: From Llynfi Junction to the Llynvi Vale Iron Works. (From the records of R.A. Cooke, Oxford.) This siding connecting line is to be seen on the map of the Llynvi Valley Railway, November 1859. (B. Richards - The History of the Llynfi Valley.)
Note 5. Mid Glamorgan Railways. Glamorgan Gazette, 1st July 1966.
Note 6. E.T. MacDermot – History of the Great Western Railway.
Note 7. B. Richards – History of the Llynvi Valley.

SOURCES OF INFORMATION:
Thomas Bevan - The railways of Mid-Glamorgan. Glamorgan Gazette, Friday 1st July 1966.
S. Richards - The Llynfi and Ogmore Railway. Norwich, 1977.
L.S. Higgins - John Brogden & Sons. *In* The Glamorgan Historian, Vol. 10, Stewart Williams, 1974.
Brinley Richards - The History of the Llynfi Valley. D. Brown & Sons, 1982.
E.T. MacDermot - History of the Great Western Railway. London, 1927. (Revised C.R. Clinker, 1964.)

3. The Ogmore Valley Connection

In order to obtain an outlet for their coal in the Ogmore Valley, the enterprising Brogden family, together with other industrialists in the area, procured an Act of Parliament on 13th July 1863 to construct a railway from Tondu through Brynmenyn and Blackmill to Nantymoel. The railway, known as the Ogmore Valley Railway, was seven miles in length, of narrow gauge, and connected with the L.V.R. at Tondu Junction. The Act also gave the company power to lay a third rail over the existing broad gauge track of the L.V.R. from Tondu to Porthcawl, thus accommodating their narrow gauge trains over the broad gauge sections. The line was officially opened for the working of mineral traffic from Nantymoel to Porthcawl on the 1st August 1865.[1]

As there was no railway in the parallel Garw Valley, the same Act of 1863 sanctioned the construction of an inclined railway over the Llangeinor mountain for the haulage of coal from the Garw Valley to join the O.V.R. line just north of Blackmill.[2]

Further coalmining developments by the Brogdens in the Ogmore Valley at this time prompted the O.V.R. Company to consider an alternative outlet for the expected increase in traffic, as the old tidal dock at Porthcawl had become ill equipped and was too small. However, the involvement of the two gauges prevented an outlet by way of the interchange station at Stormy, over the broad gauge S.W.R.[3] To overcome the problem the O.V.R. decided to join forces with the L.V.R. with whom they had a very close working relationship (because of Messrs Brogden's interests in both lines), to seek parliamentary power to construct a new dock at Porthcawl.

Thus in June 1864 the two companies procured an Act of

18

Parliament to promote the New Porthcawl Dock, and the dock itself, which cost £250,000 to complete, was opened on 22nd July 1867. The engineer who carried out the reconstruction work was R.P. Brereton who at one time had been the celebrated Isambard Kingdom Brunel's chief assistant.[3]

The passing of the Ogmore Valley Railway's Act of 28th June 1866 sanctioned the company to construct a branch line to the Garw Valley. However, as a result of a general depression in trade, the scheme was long delayed, and it was not until 25th October 1876 that a branch line was finally opened to Blaengarw at the head of the Garw Valley.[5]

Mention might be made, too, that in the same year as the O.V.R. opened their line from Nantymoel to Porthcawl (1865), they acquired the broad gauge Ely Valley Extension Railway, with powers to construct a broad gauge line from Gellyrhaidd through Hendreforgan to Gilfach Goch. This line opened for mineral traffic on 16th October 1865 and was worked by the G.W.R. as part of the Ely Valley line.[4]

The construction of a further extension by the O.V.R., from Blackmill in the Ogmore Valley to Hendreforgan, was not viable at that time, due to the operation of broad gauge tracks by the G.W.R. Hence the O.V.R. remained detached from their E.V.E.R. line until a branch of standard gauge (4'8") was opened between Blackmill and Hendreforgan on 1st September 1875[4], by which time the G.W.R. had changed to narrow gauge.

Note 1. D.S.M. Barrie - A regional history of the railways of Great Britain. Vol. 12, South Wales.

Note 2. Thomas Bevan - The railways of Mid-Glamorgan. Glamorgan Gazette, Friday, 1st July 1966.

Note 3. L.S. Higgins - John Brogden & Sons. In The Glamorgan Historian, Vol. 10, Stewart Williams, 1974.

Note 4. E.T. MacDermot - History of the Great Western Railway. London, 1927. (Revised C.R. Clinker, 1964.)

Note 5. S. Richards - The Llynvi and Ogmore Railway. Norwich, 1977.

TRACK LAYOUT IN THE UPPER LLYNFI VALLEY

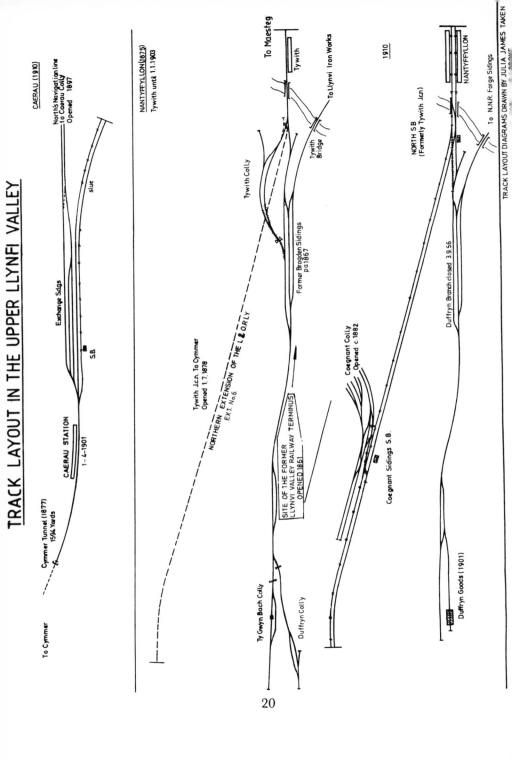

CAERAU (1910)

North's Navigation line
to Caerau Colly
Opened 1897

Exchange Sidgs

slue

S.B.

CAERAU STATION

1-4-1901

To Cymmer

Cymmer Tunnel (1877)
1594 Yards

NANTYFFYLLON(1875)
Tywith until 1.1.1903

Tywith Jcn. To Cymmer
Opened 1.7.1878

NORTHERN EXTENSION OF THE L&ORLY
Ext. No.6

SITE OF THE FORMER
LLYNVI VALLEY RAILWAY TERMINUS
OPENED 1861

To Maesteg

Tywith

To Llynvi Iron Works

Tywith
Bridge

Tywith Colly

Former Brogden Sidings
pa1867

Coegnant Colly
Opened c. 1882

Coegnant Sidings S.B.

Ty Gwyn Bach Colly

Duffryn Colly

1910

NORTH S.B.
(Formerly Tywith Jcn)

NANTYFFYLLON

To N.N.R. Forge Sidings

Duffryn Branch closed 3.9.56

Duffryn Goods (1901)

TRACK LAYOUT DIAGRAMS DRAWN BY JULIA JAMES TAKEN

20

TRACK LAYOUT IN THE UPPER LLYNFI VALLEY. Cont'd.

LLYNVI JCN (1880)

1910

Maesteg Iron Works

p a 7.4.1866

Llynvi Iron Works

MAESTEG

To St. Johns Colliery

MAESTEG
DEEP COLLIERY

S.B. N.N.R.

N.N.R
ENGINE SHEDS

Port Talbot R.ly. opened 1897

c 1901 R & a 5.4.1900

To Llynvi Iron Works

p & a 1.9.1859

LLYNVI JCN S.B.

NORTHS NAVIGATION R'LY

Colliery Lines
into use c 1890

G.W.R. LLYNFI BRANCH

Ballast Sidings
By 1925

WAGON REPAIR SHOPS
Built 1925.

N.N.R. FORGE SIDINGS

LLYNVI JCN S.B.

TO DUFFRYN
BRANCH SIDINGS

TRACK LAYOUT DIAGRAMS DRAWN BY JULIA JAMES. TAKEN
FROM ORIGINALS. BY COURTESY OF R.A.COOKE

21

4. The Llynvi and Ogmore Railway

As a result of the Ogmore Valley Railway Act of 28th June 1866, the Llynvi and Ogmore Railway Company was formed, by the amalgamation of the broad gauge L.V.R. and the standard gauge O.V.R. A standard gauge was decided upon and by 1868 a third rail had been laid to accommodate standard gauge trains over the broad gauge sections. The L.V.R. at the time exchanged three broad gauge engines and two carriages for four standard gauge engines and nine carriages from the W. Cornwall Railway. The G.W.R. broad gauge wagons continued in use over the lines until broad gauge tracks were entirely removed from South Wales in 1872.[1]

During the interim period between 1868 and 1872 the L.& O. Railway used a narrow gauge station alongside the G.W.R. platform at Bridgend Station.

Tondu junction became the headquarters of the L. & O.R. Co. A locomotive shed and workshops were erected and Mr. J. Routledge was appointed the Locomotive Superintendent.

Early Railway Developments in the Llynfi Valley.

An agreement[2] dated 7th April 1867, between the L. & O.R. Co. and the Llynvi Vale Iron Company Ltd., gave the former powers to construct new lines of narrow gauge track from their main line to connect with the Llynvi Iron Works. From a plan accompanying the agreement, it is seen that new sidings were proposed to be laid between the terminus of the former L.V.R. and Tywith Bridge, these being identified as Messrs. Brogden's Sidings. A branch line proceeded from these sidings to cross

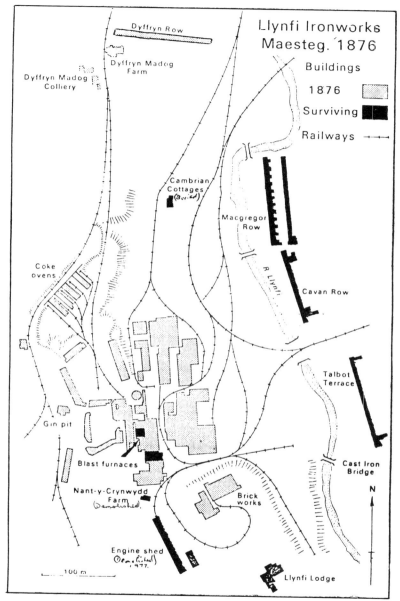

Llynfi Ironworks
Maesteg. 1876

Buildings

1876

Surviving

Railways

Dyffryn Row

Dyffryn Madog
Farm

Dyffryn Madog
Colliery

Cambrian
Cottages
(Buried)

Macgregor
Row

Coke
ovens

R Llynfi

Cavan Row

Talbot
Terrace

Gin pit

Cast Iron
Bridge

N

Blast furnaces

Nant-y-Crynwydd
Farm
(Demolished).

Brick
works

Engine shed
(Demolished)
1977.

100 m

Llynfi Lodge

(By Courtesy of Doctor Graham Humphrys, Geography Department, University of Wales, Swansea).

Tywith Bridge and then to follow the line of the old D.L. & P.R. to the Llynvi Iron Works.

From this branch a spur commenced at the bottom of Grove Street, Nantyfyllon, and proceeded along the lane below the site of the present Nantyfyllon Primary School, to connect with the Duffryn Madog colliery and then the Gin Pit (built c. 1856) which was situated on the site of the present Maesteg Recreational Park.

Also on the plan, a proposed new railway line is shown crossing the valley to connect the Llynvi Iron Works with the Maesteg Iron Works, through the construction of two bridges. The first bridge[3] crossed the main road at the bottom of Cavan Row, Maesteg, with an archway alongside it over the River Llynfi. The second crossed the L. & O. main line north of the former Maesteg Castle Street Station.

Further railway development in the Llynfi Valley is underlined by a report on the South Cwmdu colliery[4] (which was situated in the Pontrhydycyff area of the valley), made by Joshua Richardson and dated 18th April 1873. The report states: '. . . a siding line is now being constructed, which will connect the colliery with the L. & O.Rly which communicates with the S.W.R. and the railway system throughout England and Wales . . . as relates to the conveyance of the product of the colliery to the best markets for both home consumption and for exportation.'

In 1873 a Mr. Colquhoun laid before the Cwmdu Board of Health a plan showing the route of an intended railway from the Maesteg Iron Works to connect with the L. & O.R. line at a point alongside the old bridge at Castle Street. The plan was approved by the Board and the railway is seen on the 1876 O.S. map.[5]

The Northern Extension of the Llynvi and Ogmore Railway

In July 1873 the Llynvi and Ogmore Railway Company procured an Act of Parliament to allow them to construct an extension of their railway from Tywith to Abergwynfi at the head of the Afan Valley. This Act also confirmed an agreement dated 16th May 1873 between the L. & O.R. Company and the G.W.R. whereby the latter would work and manage the Llynvi and Ogmore line, and which guaranteed to the ordinary shareholders 6% on their shares in the old company.

This Northern Extension of the L. & O.R. entered the Afan Valley through a single bore tunnel at Caerau, completed in 1877, and on the 1st July 1878 the line was opened through to the village of Cymmer in the Afan Valley and thence up the valley to Abergwynfi. On the same day a junction was opened with the South Wales Mineral Line at Cymmer by means of a single span lattice girder bridge across the River Afan.

The tunnel[6], known as the Maesteg Tunnel, was 1,594 yards in length and had been driven from both ends. Work began at the Cymmer end in April 1875, and this was driven by hand labour, while the work from the Caerau side commenced in August 1875, and was chiefly carried out by machine drills. Both sides met with perfect lines and levels on 29th May 1877.

D.R. Waldin's essay on Caerau's past in the Glamorgan Advertiser, 1st July 1927, states that 'During the construction of the tunnel, wooden huts were erected along what is today Caerau Road, but was then green fields, to house the Irish workmen employed in the building of the tunnel.' Again, D.R. Waldin, in his article on the memories of Caerau, wrote that bricks from a brickworks which stood on the mountainside near Duffryn Level, were used as part of the construction of Maesteg Tunnel.

On the 27th April 1876 a very regrettable accident occurred at the Cymmer end of the tunnel, in which thirteen lives were lost by an explosion of dynamite 176 yards from the tunnel mouth where the charges were being prepared. Most of the men killed were inside the tunnel.

The datestone, marked 1877, is still to be seen on top of the archway on the Caerau side. The line from Tywith Station to Caerau had a steep gradient, rising to 1 in 37, which entailed a very heavy pull for the locomotive.

The imminent arrival of the railway at Abergwynfi occasioned the sinking of the Western Colliery at that place, this being the result of a decision by the G.W.R. Company to have its own supply of steam coal. Hence in 1877 Sir Daniel Gooch[1], the Chairman of the G.W.R. at that time, arrived in the district on horseback to cut the first sod for the sinking of the two shafts. A mineral line was then laid to connect the colliery with the main line. However, working of the colliery was intermittent, the output being restricted by several cross measure drifts which had to be driven, and eventually this led to the colliery being sold to the Ocean Coal Company in 1910/12. After the G.W.R. had sold the colliery, the miners and their families continued to receive cheap

PLAN OF THE PROPOSED OGMORE DOCK AND RAILWAY,
WITH THE COALFIELDS NORTH OF BRIDGEND.

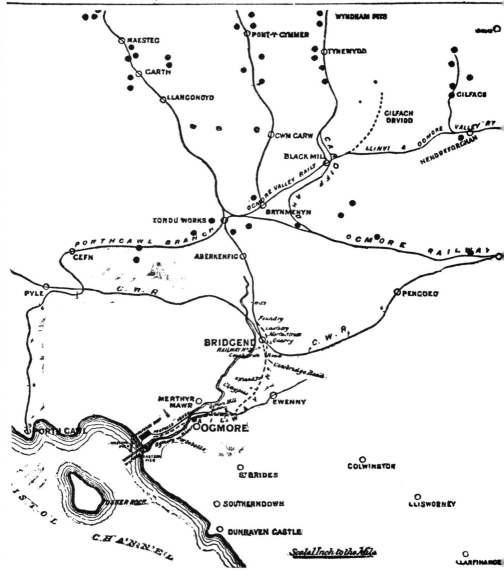

(Courtesy Glamorgan Gazette, September 29th, 1950). This plan would have transformed Mid Glamorgan. (Recorded in the 'Bridgend Chronicle', Friday, June 8th, 1883).

26

fares, similar to other railway employees at that time.[7]

The line from Tywith to Cymmer (G.W.R.) Station was opened to passengers on 16th July 1880, and the service was extended to Abergwynfi on 22nd March 1886.

The Rhondda and Swansea Bay Railway came to the Afan Valley some years later, in 1890, running parallel to the G.W.R. and passing through the 3,443 yards-long Rhondda Tunnel from Blaengwynfi at the head of the Afan Valley to Blaencwm in the Rhondda Valley.

The final amalgamation between the L. & O.R. and the G.W.R. took place on 1st July 1883. The L. & O.R. was one of the earliest of the smaller private lines in South Wales to become completely absorbed by the G.W.R. prior to the groupings of 1922/23.

Mention may be made that on 20th August 1883[8] the Ogmore Dock and Railway Act was passed. It gave powers to construct a railway line from a point starting on the Llynvi and Ogmore section of the G.W.R. line above Bridgend Station to connect with a new dock to be constructed at the mouth of the River Ogmore.

The news of such an undertaking was received with much joy and fervour by the inhabitants of Bridgend. However, after initial boring operations had begun on the construction of a new dock at Ogmore-by-Sea, financial backing wavered, and the scheme was abandoned in 1888.

Later Developments on the Llynvi and Ogmore Branch of the G.W.R. in the Llynfi Valley.

After the amalgamation in 1883 the G.W.R. made considerable alterations to the old system on the Llynfi Valley line, and in 1898 a new station was opened at Maesteg. The new platform was positioned a short distance northwards from the original station near the old goods shed, and the line was doubled[9]. This station became known as Maesteg Castle Street Station on 1st July 1924.

Tywith (Tychwith) Station (opened in c. 1875), initially had one platform, but subsequently, in 1898, had both up and down platforms of longer length. Tywith Station was renamed Nantyfyllon on 1st January 1903.[9] A new G.W.R. station was also opened at Llangonoyd in 1899; the new station was renamed Llangynwyd in March 1935. Meanwhile, Troedyrhiw Garth

Station was built in the 1870s during the time when the G.W.R. was working and managing the L. & O.R., but the platform was lengthened in 1910, and shortened again in 1938.[9]

Duffryn Goods Yard[10], which was situated near the site of the old terminus of the former Llynvi Valley Railway at Coegnant Station, was opened c. 1901. Caerau Station, at the head of the line in the Llynfi Valley, was the last station to be opened, on 1st April 1901, along with the development of the Caerau district at the turn of the nineteenth century. In the same year (1901) the main section of the line from Tondu to Bridgend was doubled. Finally, with the opening of the Blaengarw Station on 26th May 1902, a full passenger service was provided for the three valleys – Llynfi, Garw and Ogmore - converging at Tondu.

Porthcawl Dock at the Turn of the Century

The poor approach to Porthcawl Dock, together with its inadequate facilities, once more made it impossible for the site to compete economically with other South Wales ports, especially as larger steamships were coming into use. Hence at the turn of the century the dock virtually ceased to function as a port, and it was closed by the G.W.R. in 1906. Porthcawl town developed as a seaside resort with a new railway station built on the site of the old dock lines in March 1916[11], and during the years of the Second World War the dock was filled in, and later used as a car park.

It may also be mentioned that the first Sunday excursion train from Maesteg to Porthcawl ran on 15th August 1909. In his book 'The History of the Llynfi Valley', Brinley Richards gives an interesting account of the implications of travelling on a Sunday, as at that time Sabbath keeping in the valley was absolute. He states that 'The first Sunday excursion train from Maesteg to Porthcawl caused great consternation. Local ministers gathered at the Maesteg railway station to try to dissuade the offenders from travelling . . . An emergency meeting of the local churches was called to request the G.W.R. to refrain from running the Sunday trains, rather than threaten the travellers.'

The Groupings of the Railways in 1922

The curtailment of train services and the restrictions of passenger traffic during the years of the First World War, together with the labour troubles afterwards, were anxious times for the G.W.R. and the other big companies, times which culminated with the Railways Act of 1921.[12] This Act decreed that all private companies in South Wales should become completely absorbed by the G.W.R. The first of the amalgamations took effect on 1st January 1922 and contributed to a passenger connecting service with the former L. & O.R. and the former R. & S.B.R. at Cymmer, the result of which provided a through service from the Llynfi Valley to the Rhondda via the tunnel at the head of the Afan Valley.

In the same year Tondu Junction[13] was appointed by the G.W.R. to be one of the chief traffic controls in South Wales. In 1927 it had sheds for 40 engines, employed 400 railwaymen and had to deal with the output of 24 collieries from the districts of Cefn, Garw, Ogmore, Gilfach Goch, Heol-y-Cyw and the Llynfi Valley.

Like most similar lines, the former L. & O.R. line in the Llynfi Valley was severely hit during the years of the Second World War as it was during the First World War. Passenger services were limited, and the line provided mainly for miners' trains, mineral traffic and schools' services. Children from the Afan Valley and those at the top of the Llynfi Valley who were successful in the entrance examination for the Secondary School, travelled to Maesteg Castle Street Station to attend the Maesteg Secondary School (later the Grammar School), which was situated where the Llynfi Girls Comprehensive School is today. Many men from the Llynfi Valley at that time worked in the pits of the adjoining Afan Valley and travelled to work via the Maesteg Tunnel.[14]

Again, during the years of the Second World War, hundreds of workers from both the Afan and Llynfi Valleys who were employed at the 'Arsenal', the ammunitions factory that was situated on the site of the present Bridgend Industrial Trading Estate, travelled on the line to the platform at Tremains which was situated alongside the 'Arsenal'.

After the Second World War the former L. & O.R. line resumed all its old activities with renewed vigour up to, and after, the nationalisation of the railways in 1948. Sunday excursions were resumed during the Summer months to Porthcawl via Tondu, and excursions were started to the Ninian Park Halt from Tondu so that enthusiastic supporters could follow the fortunes of Cardiff City Football Club. These excursions were looked

---

ASSOCIATION FOOTBALL—ENGLISH LEAGUE DIVISION ONE

Cardiff City v Aston Villa

AT NINIAN PARK, CARDIFF.   KICK-OFF 7.15 p.m.

FOOTBALL EXCURSION

WEDNESDAY
7th SEPTEMBER, 1960

TO

NINIAN PARK
HALT

FROM	DEPART	RETURN FARES, SECOND CLASS
	p.m.	s.d.
TONDU	5 48	3/6
BRIDGEND	5 57	3/0
PENCOED	6 5	3/0
LLANHARAN	6 14	2/10
LLANTRISANT	6 23	2/5
NINIAN PARK HALT .. .. arr.	6 45	

Return train will leave Ninian Park Halt immediately after the match. Passengers may also return from Cardiff (Gen.) station the same day by any train.

Children under three years of age, free ; three and under fourteen years of age, half-fare. Fractions of a 1d. will be reckoned as a 1d.

The usual conditions of issue will apply

For further Information, apply to Stations, or to Mr. J. H. F. Page, District Traffic Superintendent Cymric Buildings, Cardiff Docks ; Telephone Cardiff 21021, Extension 713 ; or Mr. R. L. Charlesworth, Commercial Officer, Paddington Station, W.2.

Paddington Station, W.2.   **J. R. HAMMOND**

August, 1960.   General Manager.

Printed in Great Britain by Commercial & Sporting Printers Ltd., Cardiff.   TXE/6661C/HD

WESTERN (BRITISH RAILWAYS) REGION

ASSOCIATION FOOTBALL — WORLD CUP
WALES v SPAIN
At NINIAN PARK, CARDIFF   KICK-OFF 6.30 p.m.

FOOTBALL EXCURSION

WEDNESDAY

19th APRIL, 1961

TO

NINIAN PARK HALT

FROM	DEPART	RETURN FARES SECOND CLASS	Arrival on Return
	p.m.	s. d.	p.m.
TONDU	5 18	3/6	9 25
BRIDGEND	5 26	3/0	9 17
PENCOED	5 34	3/0	9 11
LLANHARAN	5 43	2/10	9 2
LLANTRISANT	5 51	2/5	8 53
NINIAN PARK HALT .. arr.	6 7		

Return Train will leave Ninian Park Halt at 8.35 p.m.
Passengers may also return from Cardiff (Gen.) Station the same day by any train.

Children under three years of age, free; three and under fourteen years of age, half-fare.
(Fractions of a 1d. will be charged as a 1d.)

NO CAR PARKING PROBLEMS IF YOU TRAVEL BY TRAIN

Further Information will be supplied on application to: Stations; Mr. J. H. F. Page, District Traffic Superintendent, Room 161, Marland House, Central Square, Cardiff (Telephone: Cardiff 21021, Ext. 445); or Mr. W. R. Stevens, Divisional Traffic Manager, Marland House, Central Square, Cardiff.

Paddington Station, W.2.   **J. R. HAMMOND,**
   March, 1961.   *General Manager*

Printed in Great Britain by Commercial & Sporting Printers Ltd., Cardiff   EP/6873C/HD

31

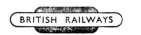
INTERNATIONAL ASSOCIATION FOOTBALL MATCH

WALES v SCOTLAND

AT NINIAN PARK, CARDIFF   KICK-OFF 3.0 p.m.

FOOTBALL EXCURSION

SATURDAY

22nd OCTOBER, 1960

TO

NINIAN PARK
HALT

FROM	DEPART	RETURN FARES, SECOND CLASS
	p.m.	s.d.
TONDU	1 0	3/6
BRIDGEND	1 8	3/0
PENCOED	1 16	3/0
LLANHARAN	1 25	2/10
LLANTRISANT	1 34	2/5
NINIAN PARK HALT .. .. arr.	1 55	

Return train will leave Ninian Park Halt immediately after the match. Passengers may also return from Cardiff (Gen.) station the same day by any train.

Children under three years of age, free ; three and under fourteen years of age, half-fare. Fractions of a 1d. will be reckoned as a 1d.

TICKETS CAN BE OBTAINED IN ADVANCE AT BOOKING STATIONS AND AGENCIES.

Further information will be supplied on application to stations; Mr. J. H. F. Page, District Traffic Superintendent, Marland House, Central Square, Cardiff. (Telephone : Cardiff 21021) ; or Mr. R. L. Charlesworth, Commercial Officer, Paddington Station, W.2.

Paddington Station, W.2.   **J. R. HAMMOND,**
September, 1960.   General Manager.

Printed in Great Britain by Commercial & Sporting Printers Ltd., Cardiff.   TXE/6719C/HD

forward to with much excitement by the inhabitants of the valley, and hundreds travelled on them during those weekends. The late night train on Saturdays, i.e. the 11.10 p.m. from Bridgend to Abergwynfi in the Afan Valley, known generally in the district as the 'Rodney', played an important part in the link between the Afan and Llynfi Valleys. In the early 1950s large numbers of passengers travelled on it. The majority of them boarded the train at Maesteg after enjoying the social amenities afforded them by the town, and some 250-300 people would alight from the train at Cymmer. The train was usually longer than the platform, and it had to pull up a second time to allow passengers in the rear of the train to alight before it could continue on its journey to Abergwynfi.

Note 1. E.T. MacDermot - History of the Great Western Railway. London, 1927.
Note 2. County Records Office, Cardiff - Reference N.C.B. 145/99/2.
Note 3. The bridge that crossed the main road at Cavan Row, Maesteg, was demolished in February 1983 for a road widening scheme.
Note 4. County Records Office, Cardiff.
Note 5. County Records Office, Cardiff - Minutes of Cwmdu Board of Health, 1873.
Note 6. G.F.Adams - Paper on Maesteg Tunnel, 1878/9.
Note 7. John Hosegood - The Great Western Colliery: Avon Colliery, Blaengwynfi. Afan Uchaf, Vol. IV, 1981.
Note 8. Glamorgan Gazette, September 29th, 1950. 'This plan would have transformed Mid-Glamorgan'. (Originally recorded in the Bridgend Chronicle, Friday, June 8th 1883.)
Note 9. R.A. Cooke - Track layout diagrams of the Llynfi Valley, Section 49.
Note 10. The old Duffryn Goods Yard is today the site of the Co-operative Supermarket at Hermon Road, Caerau.
Note 11. D.S.M. Barrie - A Regional History of the Railways of Great Britain. Vol. 22, South Wales. David and Charles, 1980.
Note 12. E.T. MacDermot - History of the Great Western Railway. Vol. 2, 1863-1921.
Note 13. Thomas Bevan - Dissertation, 1928. Glamorgan Gazette, 1st July 1966.
Note 14. The Maesteg Tunnel was known as the Cymmer Tunnel in later years.

SOURCES OF INFORMATION
Thomas Bevan M.A. - Thesis, 1928. Glamorgan Gazette, 1st July, 1966.
L.S. Higgins - The Brogdens. In The Glamorgan Historian, Vol. 10, Stewart Williams, 1974.
S. Richards - The Llynvi and Ogmore Railway. Norwich, 1977.
E.T. MacDermot - The History of the Great Western Railway. London, 1927.
D.S.M. Barrie - A Regional History of the Railways of Great Britain. Vol. 12, South Wales. David & Charles, 1980.
B. Richards - The history of the Llynfi Valley. D. Brown & Sons, 1982.
R.A. Cooke - Track Layout Diagrams of the Llynfi Valley. Oxford, 1974.
D.S.M. Barrie - Railways of the Bridgend District. In The Railway Magazine, July 1955.

5. The Port Talbot Railway (1897-1964)

The Port Talbot Railway and Docks Company was incorporated on 31st July 1894, with powers to enlarge and modernise the Port Talbot docks and to construct a railway to connect with the coal producing districts of both the Llynfi and Garw Valleys, thus superseding the earlier inclined tramway, built in 1841[1], that ran from the village of Bryn to Cwmavon.

The company was promoted by local businessmen and colliery owners who had become frustrated by the inadequacies of the tidal harbour at Porthcawl. Two[2] prominent industrial promoters at the time were Colonel J.T. North of North's Navigation Collieries in the Llynfi Valley and J.E. Watson, director of the Ffaldau Colliery in the Garw Valley. Understandably, both men were looking for an alternative outlet for their mineral resources, especially as progress on the construction of the Vale of Glamorgan Railway[3], with its terminus at the proposed new harbour at Barry, was so slow. (It ultimately took eight years to complete from its inception in 1889.)

The most influential promoters of the P.T.R. & Dock Co. were Miss Emily Charlotte (whose family name had been given to the new port - 'Port Talbot' - in 1837), the Earl of Dunraven, and Colonel Wright, the chairman of Wright, Butler & Co.[2]

By 1898 the P.T.R. & Dock Co. consisted of dock lines and three branch lines: a branch from Port Talbot to the Garw Valley; a branch that connected with the South Wales Mineral Railway at Tonmawr; and another that connected with the G.W.R. at Cefn Junction (near Tondu)[4]. This made a total of 33½ miles, as well as which an Act of 1896 permitted an eight-mile extension of the P.T.R. together with an agreement to have running powers over

G.W.R. lines to connect with traffic from the Ogmore Valley.[2]

The main traffic yard and locomotive depot was situated at Duffryn (later, c. 1922, called Duffryn Yard), today the site of a private housing estate. The first locomotive superintendent was W.J. Hosgood, who hailed from the Barry Railway, where he was assistant to his brother who was that company's locomotive and carriage superintendent. This led to a close working relationship between the two said companies for a number of years.

The P.T.R. line was opened for goods traffic from Port Talbot Central Station through Maesteg to Lletty Brongu on 31st August 1897. The line was then extended to Pontyrhyll Junction in the Garw Valley, and was opened for goods traffic on 17th January 1898.

The line was officially opened to carry passengers from Port Talbot Central Station to Pontyrhyll Junction on 14th February 1898. It is said[2] that the first train took 39 minutes for a journey of just over 14 miles.

The village of Bryn was connected to the town of Maesteg for passenger traffic with the opening of the Bryn Station in c.1899.[2] The stations on the line were: its terminal, Port Talbot Central (situated behind the Plaza Cinema); Bryn; Maesteg (Neath Road); Garth; Lletty Brongu; Bettws Llangeinor and Pontyrhyll Junction. The passenger service was extended to Blaengarw, running over G.W.R. lines, with the opening of the station at that place on 26th May 1902.

Cwmdu Station was opened in June 1913, replacing Garth Station which was closed on the same day. Cwmdu Station was situated some 46 chains westward of the old Garth Station.[5]

It is interesting to note that Lletty Brongu Station initially had two platforms; the up platform was only in operation until c. 1906 when it was taken out of use when a new crossing loop was constructed at Garth. The company's general office adjoined the Custom House near the Port Talbot Central Station, and the company's initials (P.T.R.D.C.) are still to be seen cut in the stonework of the building.

The Construction of the Line

The building of the line was indeed an engineering feat, which entailed following a very tortuous route up a steep, narrow ravine. The construction of a tunnel 1010 yards in length, and the building of a viaduct 114 yards long and 73 feet high, were followed by a cutting through very hard rock which circled around the brow of the Moelgilau mountain. The Irish workmen employed on this section - known locally as the Moelgilau gap - were housed in temporary wooden huts alongside the line at Bettws Llangeinor during the time of its construction.

The whole length of the line was 14 miles, 1 chain.

The Route of the Line

Turning eastward from Port Talbot (Central) Station, the line ran along the edge of the Aberavon Athletic Football Ground and led to the traffic yard and depot at Duffryn, situated at the mouth of the Goytre Valley (or Duffryn Valley). There it swung northwards up the narrow valley to the village of Bryn, with a continuously rising gradient of 1 in 40 for 3 ½ miles until it entered Cwmcerwin tunnel.[6] The datestone, inscribed P.T.R. 1897, is still to be seen on both sides of this tunnel. From there the railway passed through the Sychbant Valley, nestling peacefully below Margam Mountain, before it swung around the town of Maesteg, avoiding the G.W.R. tracks. The line skirted the Maesteg R.F.C. ground, the embankment of which was strategically placed so as to allow those who ventured to trespass a splendid view of matches played on the ground. At this point the line crossed to the eastern side of the valley by way of two bridges, one that crossed over the main road and another that crossed over the G.W.R. main line. (As already mentioned, these bridges were built c. 1867, to connect the Maesteg Iron Works with the Llynvi Iron Works.) At the time of the construction of the P.T.R. both bridges were owned by North's Navigation Collieries, a company having interests in the P.T.R.

The line served collieries on the eastern side of the Llynfi Valley as far as Bettws (Llangeinor Station). Along this stretch it emerged upon the entrance of the picturesque Darran Valley, a local beauty spot, crossing this valley via a viaduct of imposing grandeur, 114 yards long and 73 feet high, with seven arches of 40 foot span and one of 20 foot span.[3] This viaduct, built of red brick, is known as the Pontrhydycyff[7] viaduct, and still stands today, reminding one of the railway development in that region of the Llynfi Valley.

After leaving the viaduct, the line circled the brow of the

36

mountain to the Moelgilau gap before turning northwards up the Garw Valley. Along this section it passed through farmland, which required the construction of a number of cattle archways to allow cattle access from one pasture to another. Finally the line crossed the River Garw via a small bridge ahead of Pontyrhyll Junction.

The 1 in 40 ascent on the western side of Cwmcerwin tunnel was understandably a very heavy pull for the locomotive. In order to overcome this problem the P.T.R. purchased two 0-8-2 engines, Nos. 20 and 21, from the Cooke Locomotive Co. of Paterson, New Jersey. These engines were known as the 'Yankee Engines'. In connection with this fierce stretch of the line there was a run-away safety end constructed at Tyn-y-Ffram in the Duffryn Valley.

The section of the line on the western side of the tunnel served the Bryn Navigation Colliery at the village of Bryn. This colliery was purchased by Messrs. Baldwins from Wright, Butler & Co. in 1902, for £22,000. The line also served the English Celluloid Co. Works from 1902 to 1906; these works were situated above the village of Goytre in the Duffryn Valley. From 1919 the line served the Cwm Gwineu Colliery (later called the Glenhavod Collieries), which was also situated in the Duffryn Valley, in addition to which the P.T.R., for many of its earlier years, served the brick works situated alongside the line 250 yards from the mouth of the Cwm Cerwin tunnel and the Ton Hir Colliery which was connected to the line by a tramway on the eastern side.

Later Developments

On the 24th January 1908 an agreement was signed between the G.W.R. and the P.T.R. for the G.W.R. to work the railway side of the Company, although the dock still remained with the P.T.R. The effect of this agreement was that the day to day management of the P.T.R. still remained with that company, although all local decisions were subject to confirmation by the G.W.R. at Paddington. Again, the P.T.R. engines were sent to the G.W.R. works at Swindon for heavy overhaul, and some G.W.R. engines were sent down to Duffryn with effect from the date of this agreement.[8]

The Working of the Line

From the time of its construction, and for many years

thereafter, the P.T.R. proved to be a valuable connecting link between the Garw Valley, Maesteg and Port Talbot. Thousands would travel on the line to the seaside at Aberavon during the summer months. Alighting at Port Talbot Central Station, passengers would continue their journey to the beach in horse-drawn brakes with gaily coloured canopies; sadly, this more leisurely mode of town travel was replaced at the end of the 1914-18 War by motorised traffic. The open air market held every Friday at Maesteg was as popular then, if not more so, than it is today, with large numbers travelling on the line from the Garw Valley and the village of Bryn to shop at Maesteg.

Pupils from the Garw Valley who were successful in passing the scholarship examination to gain entry into the Maesteg Secondary School (opened in 1912, on the site of the present Plasnewydd Primary School), would travel on the line from Blaengarw, Pontycymmer and Pontyrhyll to the Maesteg Neath Road Station.

The popular away fixture of the Maesteg R.F.C. versus the Aberavon R.F.C. would fill the train with the team players and supporters, travelling from Neath Road Station, Maesteg, to Port Talbot Central Station (and vice versa for the return fixture at Maesteg.)

Under the powers granted by the Railway Act 1921, the docks and railways of the P.T.R. & Docks Company became completely absorbed in the G.W.R. Company as from 1st January 1922.

Closure of the Line

The construction of the new road from Maesteg through Bryn to Port Talbot, which was opened in 1926 and which was constructed under the Government Unemployment Relief scheme, resulted in the would-be rail passengers on the former P.T.R. gradually reverting to road transport. Prior to the opening of the new road to Port Talbot, the old road via Bryn was in such a bad condition (being merely a rough track) that motorised traffic going to Port Talbot had to travel via Bridgend, or over roads from Aberkenfig and Tondu to Stormy Down or Pyle to connect with the main road going west. The new route from Maesteg to Port Talbot was first operated by the Llynfi Bus Company[9] and shortly afterwards jointly with the South Wales

Transport Company. Inevitably, the opening of the new road to Port Talbot deprived the G.W.R. of part of its passenger traffic on the former P.T.R. line, and as a consequence the G.W.R. Company gradually cut back its passenger train service on the line.[10]

From 22nd September 1930 the G.W.R. public time table advertised through passenger trains to Blaengarw to run on Fridays and Saturdays only. This allowed the inhabitants of the Garw Valley th opportunity of continuing to travel to the town of Maesteg for the purpose of shopping, keeping up a practice that had been a way of life since the line initially opened for passenger traffic on 14 February 1898.

During the period at weekends when the train travelled from Maesteg Neath Road Station to Blaengarw, a porter would board the train at Maesteg to book passengers on and off the train at stations along the route to Blaengarw Station. Alas, this service connecting the two valleys was severed on 12th September 1932, much to the disappointment of the inhabitants of both valleys. On a still sadder note, 12 months later, on 11th September 1933, the passenger service between Maesteg and Port Talbot finally came to an end.

With the gradual cut-back in coal production due to the fall-off in coal exportation in the early 1930s, and because the Garw coal had long since been transported by way of the Tondu route[11] on the G.W.R. line, no traffic was worked on the line between Lletty Brongu Station and Pontyrhyll Junction during the Second World War. The section of line from Lletty Brongu Station as far as the Moelgilau gap was used for wagon storage during that period, while the remaining portion of the line to Pontyrhyll Junction was used as a siding for the G.W.R. Garw branch.

In 1947[12] the section of line between Lletty Brongu Station and Pontyrhyll Junction was severed at Bettws Llangeinor, and thus began the removal of various sections of the track between Cwmdu and Pontyrhyll. In 1948 the section of track between Bettws Llangeinor and a point within 29 chains from Pontyrhyll Junction was removed; in 1949 the track from Bettws Llangeinor to the Celtic Halt Sidings was taken up; then, eventually, in the summer of 1959 the section of line between Cwmdu and the Celtic Halt Sidings was lifted, although the section was not officially closed until 9th May 1960. In connection with this section of the line, a devastating thunderstorm occurred during the first week of August 1954, completely washing away the ballast supporting part of the track, between the Gelli Hir sidings and Lletty Brongu Station. The track was temporarily supported with additional railway sleepers, and horses hired from the nearby Gelli Hir Farm were used to haul out the empty coal wagons stored beyond Lletty Brongu Station.

The remaining section of the track at the end of the line near Pontyrhyll Junction was ultimately closed in June 1962.

A further run-down of coal traffic in the early 1960s, due to a run-down of shipments from Port Talbot Docks, resulted in the closure of the old P.T.R. from Duffryn Junction to Cwmdu, from 31st August 1964, with the exception of the section of track between the N.C.B. workshop on the site of the old Llynfi Iron Works and Cwmdu. This last remaining section of the former P.T.R. line was transferred to the N.C.B. under the British Railways Act of 27th July 1967.[13]

It is interesting to note that the P.T.R. was steam worked throughout its entire life in the Llynfi Valley.

The last freight train from Maesteg to Port Talbot (Duffryn Yard), on 28th August 1964, was hauled by Engine No. 5213 – a former G.W.R. 42XX class engine.

The following is a quotation taken from the Glamorgan Gazette newspaper for 18th September 1964:

FOR THE OLD P.T.R. IT'S THE END OF THE LINE

Twin engine whistles shrilled a piercing farewell as seventeen trucks hauled 300 tons of best Maesteg coal down the line through the old P.T.R. Station of Neath Road. It was in fact the last train to pass down the Port Talbot Railway from the Llynfi Valley; and with its departure the creation of yet another 'ghost station'.

The Line Today

The trackbed in the Duffryn Valley is today used as a bridle path, and is easily sighted; however the trackbed on the eastern side of the Cwmcerwin Tunnel is not so easy to locate, large sections having been used for housing development or for land reclamation schemes, while others have been engulfed by the tentacles of nature and are no longer traceable.

Mention may be made that the station building at Lletty Brongu has recently been converted into a dwelling house. The builder has very graciously incorporated the original tall red-brick chimney stack in the new structure, and this feature is the only remaining evidence of its ever having been a railway station building.

Note 1. A.L. Evans – The story of Taibach and district. Alun Books, 1982.
Note 2. S. Richards – Port Talbot Railway. Norwich, 1977.
Note 3. J. Page – Forgotten Railways of South Wales. David & Charles, 1979.
Note 4. E.T. MacDermot – History of the Great Western Railway. London, 1927.
Note 5. R.A. Cooke – Track Layout Diagrams, Port Talbot and Cymmer Branches (Section 51).
Note 6. Cwmcerwin Tunnel was known locally as the Bryn Tunnel.
Note 7. Pontrhydycyff Viaduct is also referred to as the Cwmdu Viaduct.
Note 8. E.R. Mountford – Personal records.
Note 9. Mrs. Ann Jones (Maesteg) – Details of early road transport in the Maesteg district.
Note 10. A. King-Davies – Local Government and Civic Affairs. Maesteg Town Hall Centenary, 1981.
Note 11. S. Richards – Port Talbot Railway. Norwich, 1977.
Note 12. R.A. Cooke – Track Layout Diagrams, Port Talbot and Cymmer Branches (Section 51).
Note 13. D.S.M. Barrie – A Regional History of the Railways of Great Britain. Vol. 12 – South Wales. David & Charles, 1980.

SOURCES OF INFORMATION
E. de la Praudiere – Port Talbot and its progress. Port Talbot Docks and Railway Company, Cardiff, 1919.
Glamorgan Gazette – 18th September 1964.
E.T. MacDermot – History of the Great Western Railway. Vol. 2, 1863-1921. (Revised C.R. Clinker).
J. Page – Forgotten Railways of South Wales. David & Charles, 1979.
D.S.M. Barrie – A Regional History of the Railways of Great Britain. Vol. 12 – South Wales. David & Charles, 1980.
S. Richards – Port Talbot Railway. Norwich, 1977.
R.A. Cooke – Track Layout Diagrams, Port Talbot and Cymmer Branches. (Section 51).
E.R. Mountford – Personal records.
A. King-Davies – Railways of the Llynfi Valley. *In* Maesteg and District Festival of Wales Souvenir Brochure, 1958.
P.T.R. Parliamentary Bills, Acts etc. Taibach Reference Library, Port Talbot.

MAESTEG & BRIDGEND CHAMBERS of TRADE

Annual Outing
To Bath ★

Wednesday, September 1st, 1948

The Train leaves Caerau at 8 a.m. and will call at NANTYFFYLLON, MAESTEG and TROEDYRHIW (Garth). The Fare will be 30/- (to be paid on Booking) which will include the following :-

Lunch at 12.30 p.m. at pre-arranged Centres
Tea at 4.15 p.m.   ,,   ,,   ,,
A Straight Play at " Theatre Royal " at 7 p.m.
Variety at " Palace Theatre " at 6.30 p.m.

Please state Play or Variety when booking

Application for seats to be made not later than 23rd August, 1948.

ENTERTAINMENTS and TOURS
(not included in fare)

1. Parties taken through Bath Abbey by Official Guide.
2. Conducted Parties to historic Houses of Bath.
3. Conducted Parties to Old Roman Bath.
4. Boating on the River Avon.

A military band will be playing in the Parade Gardens from 3 to 4-30 p.m.

Bus trips can be arranged by any interested parties to Bristol 14 1-2 miles, Bradford-on-Avon 8 1-2 miles, Norton St. Philip 7 miles. Clock at 29 miles.

Booking and enquiries should be made at the following stores :-
Mr. D. Lewis, Boot Stores, Talbot street.
Messrs. Hodges & Co., Clothiers, Talbot St
Mr J. Ace, Newsagent, Commercial St.
Mr Jenkins, Furnishers, Commercial St
Messrs Rees and Wilburs, Commercial St.
Messrs. Jones and Hughes, Furnishers, Commercial St.
Ben Jones and Co., Grocers, Caerau.

BRITISH RAILWAYS (Western Region),

EVERY SUNDAY until further notice
CHEAP DAY TICKETS
will be issued to

PORTHCAWL

FROM	at	Ret'rn Fares 3rd.cls	FROM	at	Ret'rn Fares 3rd.cls
	p.m.	s. d.		p.m.	s. d.
Nantymoel	1.40	3 6	Abergwynfi	1.10	4 5
Wyndham Halt	1.45	3 3	Cymmer (Gen.)	1.15	3 9
Ogmore Vale	1.50	3 3	Caerau	1.20	3 7
Lewistown Halt	1.55	2 10	Nantyffyllon	1.25	3 4
Blackmill	2.0	2 9	Maesteg	1.30	3 3
Blaengarw	1.40	3 4	Troedyrhiew G	1.34	2 10
Pontycymmer	1.44	3 3	Llangynwyd	1.35	2 10
Pontyrhyll	1.45	2 10	Tondu	1.45	2 1
Llangeinor	1.50	2 7	Kenfig Hill	1.55	1 3
Brynmenyn	1.55	2 4	Pyle	2.5	0 11

Return Trains leave PORTHCAWL at 8.10 p.m. for Stations to Abergwynfi and 8.45 p.m. for Tondu and Stations to Nantymoel and Blaengarw.

For Further particulars apply to any Station, Office or Agency

Glamorgan Advertiser — August 13th, 1948.

42

6. Industrial and Railway Development at the Turn of the Century

In 1889 Colonel North bought the amalgamated holdings of the Llynvi and Tondu Coal and Iron Co. Ltd. together with those held by Messrs. Brogden and Sons, and North's Navigation Collieries Ltd. was floated with a capital of £450,000.

At the time the property consisted in part of the freehold properties of No. 9 Level at Maesteg, Maesteg Deep and Coegnant Collieries. The two shafts at Coegnant Colliery had been sunk by the Llynvi and Tondu Iron Company in 1882. North's Navigation Collieries remodelled and deepened the older pits to reach the richer seams of steam coal, and opened new pits at Caerau in 1897 and St. John's (Cwmdu) in 1910.

By the early 1920s the Llynvi Valley had developed as an area of great coal production, chiefly as a result of the activities of two enterprising companies, North's Navigation Collieries and the Celtic Collieries Ltd., (formed in 1909). The companies had been helped considerably by the opening of the P.T.R. in 1897, which gave access to the Docks at Port Talbot, a distance of only 9 miles from Maesteg, and the Vale of Glamorgan Railway, opened on 1st December 1897, from Coity Junction to Barry Docks.

The extensive development in coal mining caused a rapid rise in the population of the Maesteg district. In 1891 the population was 9,417; by 1901 it had risen to 15,012 , and by 1911 it was 24,977. This rise in population in turn created an accelerated growth in the development of settlements in the district. New housing was built in Maesteg behind Commercial Street, between Llynfi Road and behind Bridgend Road, while new shops were built at Talbot Street to connect with the older shopping area along Commercial Street.[1]

The 1891 Valuation List[2] for Llangynwyd Higher states that North's Navigation Company owned the following properties in the Nantyfyllon district: Union Street, John Street, Brown Street, Forbes Place (which included part of High Street, Bangor Terrace, Grove Street and Picton Street), McGarrod Row, Spelter Yard, Metcalfe Street and a school room at Bangor Terrace. Many of these properties were originally built for the iron workers; however, most of the houses north of Metcalfe Street, that is, in the Caerau district, were built after 1890, to house coal miners and their families.

The Maesteg Internal Railway System

In order to connect its collieries with the existing railway system in the Llynfi Valley, North's Navigation Company constructed its own private railway system, the North's Navigation Railway. The Siding Line that once connected the Llynvi Iron Works with the Llynvi Junction via the bridge below the Collier's Arms at Nantyfyllon became integrated into the N.N.R. system in 1889, and likewise the line that once connected the Llynvi Iron Works with the Maesteg Deep Colliery via the bridge at the bottom of Cavan Row was integrated into the Company's internal system in 1889.

With the closure of the Ginn Pitt in c. 1877[3] and the Duffryn Madog Colliery in c. 1882, the mineral line that linked these collieries to the former Brogden Sidings at Tywith Bridge was subsequently taken out of use. However the G.W.R. Branch line that ran from the former Brogden Sidings to the old Llynvi Iron Works via Bangor Terrace and High Street at Nantyfyllon continued in use until c. 1916, its chief function being to carry coal from the new N.N.R. sidings at the 'Forge' to the Dyffryn coal yard at the head of the Coegnant Branch line.

Circa 1916 the coal yard was resited at the Forge Sidings.

The opening of the Caerau colliery in 1897 necessitated the construction of a mineral line that ran southward from that colliery to link firstly with Coegnant Colliery and then with the Maesteg Deep Colliery, from where there was a connection with the main line at Llynvi Junction and the N.N.R. siding at the 'Forge'. Coegnant Colliery had been linked to the main G.W.R. branch line since c.1882. In 1897 a siding line was also constructed by the N.N.C. to connect Caerau Colliery with the

44

main line between Caerau and Nantyfyllon.

A private siding agreement, dated 5th April 1900,[4] between the P.T.R. and the N.N.C. Company led to the laying down in 1901 of new lines to connect the N.N.R. line, which ran from the Caerau and Coegnant collieries, with the P.T.R. near the North's Collieries' signal box.

Again, the opening of St. John's (Cwmdu) colliery in 1910 occasioned the laying down of a mineral line a mile long, with a gradient varying from 1 in 25 to 1 in 40, to connect with the P.T.R. at Cwmdu sidings. In connection with this mineral line a fatal accident occurred when a locomotive which was taking 10 loaded wagons of waste down the gradient ran away and crashed into a block at the siding end, crushing a labourer. The four men on the engine jumped clear. H.M. Inspector of Mines Report for 6th October 1909 stated that the train ran wild owing to greasy rails, and a probable defect in the apparatus for supplying sand, coupled with the heavy weight of the load.

During its existence the N.N.R. had running powers over, firstly, the P.T.R. metals, and, later after the 'Grouping' of 1922, over G.W.R. metals from North's Collieries' Signal Box to Cwmdu Sidings. This practice was subsequently continued by the N.C.B. over the B.R. lines following the nationalisation of the railways in 1948.

The engine shed which once formed part of the old Llynvi Iron Works complex was used as a locomotive workshop by the N.N.R. for the maintenance of its engines and the haulage engines used in the N.N.C.'s collieries; besides this, the N.N.C. owned engineering and wagon repair shops at Tondu. In 1925 the workshops at Tondu were supplemented by the construction of a wagon repair shop at the site of the N.N.R. sidings at the 'Forge', Nantyfyllon.

The locomotives purchased by the N.N.C. for use on its internal railway system took the names of the daughters of the Company's officials. Though this practice was not unique to the N.N.R., past employees of the N.N.C. remember the names of the Company's locomotives with pride. The names of the earlier locomotives of the Company were Celia, Antonia, Carmen, Emma and Marion; the list was then interrupted by one locomotive, No. 15, with the initials J.L. Ltd., which was purchased from J. Lysaght, Frodingham. The last new locomotive purchased by the N.N.C. was named Eileen.[5] The merger of the N.N.C. with the Powell Dyffryn Company in 1945/6 saw this practice being carried on with the naming of 'Patricia'.

Old traditions die hard, and the practice continued with the nationalisation of the coal mines in August 1947. The locomotives that were purchased by the N.C.B. during the early years of nationalisation, for use on the Maesteg internal railway system, were ex War Department engines that had been rebuilt; of these, Norma and Linda were purchased in 1952 and Pamela in 1956. A new locomotive received by the N.C.B. in 1962 was named Maureen on 20th July 1964, Maureen being the name of the daughter of Mr. J. Blackmore who was the N.C.B. group engineer for the Maesteg collieries and the Maesteg internal railway system at the time.

The internal railway system in the Maesteg district became dieselised with the arrival, on 7th June 1973, of the first diesel, No. G.E.C. 5368, which was put into operation almost immediately. However, steam locomotives were still worked on the internal railway system for the following four years. Initially they worked alongside the diesel engines, but they were gradually withdrawn and were later used as a standby for diesel breakdowns. Eventually three of the last four remaining steam locomotives were sold for preservation, moving first to Bitton near Bristol on 28th March 1977. The fourth, named Pamela, was held in reserve. At the time of writing, Maureen and W. Bagnall 2766 are on the Dart Valley Railway, Buckfastleigh, where Maureen has been restored to working order. Linda is on the Kent and East Sussex Railway, awaiting restoration.[5]

The engine shed on the site of the old Llynvi Iron Works was closed in November 1975 when the working locomotives were moved to the new diesel shed built at the Maesteg Washery.[6] The old engine shed at the 'Forge' site was finally demolished in 1977.

The Forge siding closed in the early 1960s, when the new coalyard was opened at the Maesteg Washery. By 1965 the site was cleared by the Maesteg Urban District Council for the Development of light industry.

The Decline in Coal Mining in the Maesteg District.

In 1922 the N.N.C. took control over the whole of the Llynfi Valley coal output, with the exception of small levels. For the next five years or so the Maesteg district continued to flourish as a coal production area, and by the mid 1920s Garth and Oakwood Collieries were producing a combined annual output of 250,000 tons of coal,[7] while the district as a whole produced over a million tons annually. Then, in 1928, an economic depression began which was to continue through the 1930s, as a result of which many of the collieries in the Maesteg district closed. The Oakwood Colliery closed in 1928, Maesteg Deep in 1929 and Garth Pit in 1930. After this time only three collieries remained working in the district: Caerau, Coegnant and St. John's. Sadly, Caerau closed in 1977, followed by Coegnant in November 1981, leaving only St. John's as the last remaining colliery affording employment in the Maesteg area today.

Note 1.   Dr. Graham Humphreys – The industrial history of Maesteg. 1981.
Note 2.   County Record Office – Valuation List for Llangynwyd Higher, 1891.
Note 3.   Brinley Richards – The history of the Llynfi Valley.
Note 4.   R.A. Cooke – Track Layout of the Llynfi Valley. (Section 49).
Note 5.   R.L. Pittard *and* J. O'Flynn – Details of the Maesteg Internal Railway System.
Note 6.   Maesteg Washery was built c.1957.
Note 7.   Mrs. Lynne Self – Details of the Coal Industry of the Llynfi Valley.

SOURCES OF INFORMATION
Dr. Graham Humphreys – The industrial history of Maesteg. Maesteg Town Hall Centenary Brochure, 1981.

Brinley Richards – History of the Llynfi Valley, D. Brown & Sons, 1982.

R.A. Cooke – Track Layout Diagrams of the Llynfi Valley. (Section 49). 1974.

J. O'Flynn – Notes on the Maesteg internal railway system.

R.L. Pittard – Details of the Maesteg internal railway system.

Valuation List for Llangynwyd Higher, 1891. County Record Office.

Registrar General – Census Returns, 1891, 1901, 1911.

7. Withdrawals on the Former Llynvi and Ogmore Railway

The development of the railway system in the Llynfi Valley was common to that of other South Wales valleys. It ran parallel with the development of the coal and iron industries, and the early railways satisfied a need for transporting goods to the coast; but in later years as the coal industry began to decline, so did the importance of the railways.

The 1961 census revealed that the population of the Maesteg district was 21,625. This was nearly 8,000 less than the figures for 1931, and the reduction can be explained by the cutbacks in the coal industry, followed by people leaving the area to seek employment elsewhere. Meanwhile advances in road construction and in the production of motor vehicles made transport by road a serious rival to the railways. As a result passenger services were gradually cut back and stations were closed on many of the South Wales valley lines.

On 13th June 1960 Abergwynfi Station, at the head of the former L. & O.R. Extension line in the Afan Valley, was closed to passenger traffic. However, the service continued via Cymmer Afan Station to Blaengwynfi Station over the former L. & O.R. Extension tracks as far as Gelli Junction, where a new line was constructed to the former R. & S.B.R. line. Goods traffic continued to use the Abergwynfi Station until 27th May 1963. On 3rd December 1962 a new passenger route was introduced in the Afan Valley. The Treherbert to Swansea passenger service on the former R. & S.B.R. was withdrawn, and replaced by a new diesel rail car service between Treherbert and Bridgend over the rearranged lines at Cymmer.[1]

Steam traction on passenger trains continued in use from

Bridgend to Blaengwynfi Station until 1st December 1962, after which time it was replaced by diesel rail cars which consisted of a single unit for most services. Steam freight trains continued to run up the Llynfi Valley until early 1965, although after 18th April 1964 most of the freight trains were hauled by diesel locomotives following the closure of Tondu Shed.[2]

As a result of the report of the British Railways Board, Western Region, the R. & S.B.R. in the Afan Valley was closed from Duffryn Rhondda to Aberavon and Briton Ferry in 1964. Consequently coal from Duffryn Rhondda and Tonmawr Collieries was hauled up the valley to Cymmer and taken to the new marshalling sidings at Margam via Tondu.[1]

On 3rd September 1956 Duffryn Goods branch line in the Llynfi Valley was closed, and its connection with the main line was taken out of use on 1st December 1957.[2]

Then, the announcement on 26th February, 1968, by the Western Region, of its decision to close the Rhondda Tunnel, marked the end of the passenger service between Cymmer and Treherbert. The service continued to operate only between Bridgend and Cymmer Afan, with a connecting bus service between Cymmer and Treorchy over the Bwlch mountain road.

On the same day, 20th February 1968, all parcel traffic at Llynfi Valley stations ended.[2]

With the closure of the last remaining colliery in the Afan Valley, South Pit (Glyncorrwg Colliery) in 1970, all freight traffic ceased beyond Caerau. In the same year the Bridgend to Cymmer passenger service was withdrawn by the British Railways Board, Western Region; the last passenger train travelled down the Llynfi Valley line to Bridgend on Saturday, 20th June 1970. However school trains continued to run to Llangynwyd Station until the end of term, being 14th July 1970, the official closure date, in order to serve the recently established Maesteg Senior Comprehensive School.[3] Alas, this was the end of a passenger train service in the Llynfi Valley which first commenced on 25th February 1864. Sadly, the closure also severed the rail link between the Afan and Llynfi Valleys which began with the opening of the Maesteg Tunnel in 1878.

The neighbouring Garw Valley had lost the Blaengarw passenger service as early as 9th February 1953, and the Ogmore Vale Branch lost the Nantymoel service on 3rd May

1958.[4] The section of line between Nantyfyllon and Caerau closed for freight traffic on 7th September 1976 and was officially closed on 7th March 1977.[5] Traffic from Caerau Colliery continued to travel via the Coegnant inlet to the Maesteg Colliery until the closure of Caerau Colliery on 27th August 1977.

Traffic lower down the line was also lost in 1977 with the closure of the Llynfi Power Station which had been opened in 1943. Further traffic was lost in 1981[2] when the Bridgend Paper Mills traffic reverted to road transport; the small mines and coal yard traffic at Maesteg station ended when Coegnant Colliery ceased production in 1981.

Today the line in the Llynfi Valley is a single track from Tondu to Nantyfyllon, serving St. John's Colliery and the Maesteg Washery, both of which are connected to the main line at Llynvi Junction. It is interesting to note that the line used by the N.C.B. from the Cwmdu sidings leading to the Maesteg Washery (a distance of just over a mile) is the last section of the former P.T.R. remaining in the Llynfi Valley.

Since the decline of the coal industry, light industry has been introduced into the area. An industrial estate stands where Oakwood Colliery once stood. The district has now been declared a Special Development Area and a new industrial site has been established on the location of the old Forge Sidings at Nantyfyllon; new factory buildings have been erected near the old Spelter's Yard at Coegnant. The population of the Maesteg district today is almost static; in the census returns of 1981 a population of 20,888 was recorded.

Bus services at present run to Bridgend, Port Talbot, Cardiff, Neath, Swansea, Cymmer, Glyncorrwg and Abergwynfi. Local bus services link Maesteg with the districts of Caerau, Nantyfyllon, Garth, Cwmfelin and Llangynwyd.

Eight years after the last passenger train service left Maesteg, the people of the Llynfi Valley had the good fortune to be able to travel once more down the Llynfi Valley line by train. On 30th September 1978 the Maesteg branch of Tenovus, the organisation for cancer research, together with members of the Maesteg Rugby Club, chartered a diesel locomotive hauled train from B.R. to travel from Maesteg Castle Street to Paddington. Six hundred people were able to enjoy this happy

experience, and the profit on ticket sales went to local charities.[6]
Long may this community spirit prevail in the Llynfi Valley!

Note 1. William Jones – The Rhondda and Swansea Bay Revisited. *In* The Railway World Magazine, March 1970.
Note 2. R.L. Pittard – Notes on the G.W.R. Llynfi Branch.
Note 3. J. Page – Forgotten Railways of South Wales. David & Charles, 1979.
Note 4. D.S.M. Barrie – A Regional History of the Railways of Great Britain. Vol. 12 – South Wales. David & Charles, 1980.
Note 5. R.A. Cooke – Track Layout Diagrams of the Llynfi Valley. 1974.
Note 6. South Wales Echo, September 30th, 1978.

SOURCES OF INFORMATION
J. Page – Forgotten Railways of South Wales. David & Charles, 1979.
D.S.M. Barrie – A Regional History of the Railways of Great Britain. Vol. 12 – South Wales. David & Charles, 1980.
R.A. Cooke – Track Layout Diagrams of the Llynfi Valley. Oxford, 1974.
R.L. Pittard – Notes on the G.W.R. Llynfi Branch.
William Jones – The Rhondda and Swansea Bay Revisited. *In* The Railway World Magazine, March 1970.
South Wales Echo – September 30th 1978.
Registrar General – Census Returns 1931, 1961.

REFLECTIONS OF THE
LLYNFI VALLEY RAILWAYS

The new Station at Llangonoyd (c. the turn of the century). This station was renamed Llangynwyd in March, 1935. The photograph shows the station master with railway staff. (By Courtesy of Mrs. D. Court, Llangynwyd).

53

I. The Duffryn Llynvi and Porthcawl Railway

The Bridge of the River Llynfi at Bridge Street. It was built in 1827, to connect the Maesteg Iron Works with the D.L. & P.R. at Garnlwyd, c.1905. (Courtesy Byron Gage, Dyffryn Rhondda).

A commemorative plaque to the Duffryn Llynvi and Porthcawl Railway Company
This stone and section of the railway stands in a stone structure adjoining the Maesteg car park near the town centre. It was unveiled in September 1971. This commemorative plaque was made possible through the joint efforts of the Maesteg Historical and Preservation Society and the Kenfig Hill and District Music and Arts Society. (Courtesy of Lynne Self, Nantyffyllon).

The inscription on the memorial stone reads as follows:—

THE DUFFRYN LLYNFI & PORTHCAWL RAILWAY COMPANY
1825—1860

This 4' 6'' gauge horsedrawn tramroad and dock at Porthcawl, completed in 1828, gave the expanding iron and coal industries of the Llynfi Valley the first outlet to the sea.

The tramroad ran from Duffryn Llynfi, along Commercial Street and Llwydarth Road, Maesteg, through Coytrahen, Tondu, Cefn Cwsc, Kenfig Hill, Tydraw and Nottage, a distance of 25 miles, including the branches to Bettws and Bridgend.

It was the only rail transport until the steam Llynfi Valley Railway Service began in 1861.

The Keystone of the 'Old Works' Bridge

The keystone of the 'Old Works' bridge is now permanently fixed in the retaining wall at the junction of Castle Street and Bridge Street, Maesteg. (Courtesy of Lynne Self, Nantyffyllon).

THE ABOVE IS THE KEYSTONE
OF THE 'OLD WORKS' BRIDGE
WHICH STOOD ON THIS SITE
AND WAS DEMOLISHED 1952

The Porthcawl Dock c.1930. It was known at the time as 'Salt Lake', and used as a boating lake and swimming pool. Today it is a car park; it was filled in during the Second World War with waste taken from Aberbaiden Colliery. (Courtesy Mr. Les Buckingham). (Mr. Buckingham, as a boy, was on this Sunday School outing from Ponthydyclff, and is seen in the photograph, seated sixth from left, wearing a boy's cap).

II. Railway Lines that served the Llynfi Valley

General view of the Maesteg district, looking south from above the ruins of Duffryn Madog Colliery, Nantyfyllon, in the 1950's. On the left can be seen coal wagons at the Forge Sidings. Coal wagons are also seen on the N.N.R. line ahead of the two bridges, built c.1867, connecting the Maesteg Iron Works with the Llynfi Iron Works, and which later carried the P.T.R. line from one side of the valley to the other.

Caerau Station. In the foreground can be seen the bridge crossing the main road, and to the right the Station Hotel, c.1920s. (Courtesy John Lyons, Maesteg).

Approaching Caerau Station from the south, c.June 1970. (Courtesy R. M. Davies, Caerau).

Caerau Station damaged by fire c.1960. In the background can be seen the Station Hotel. After the closure of the station c.1971, part of the platform structure was used on the Gwili Railway platform at Carmarthen. (Courtesy Byron Gage).

Maesteg Castle Street Station c.1970. The official notice displayed states the withdrawal of passenger rail services between Bridgend and Cymmer Afan on Monday, 22nd June, 1970. Also of interest to note is the sign which states 'Trains to Treherbert this platform. Trains to Bridgend over footbridge'. (Courtesy Dr. Lyn Jones, Maesteg).

Approaching Maesteg Castle Street from the south. Small mines coal is seen being loaded in the foreground. c.1963. (Courtesy John Morgans, Cymmer).

Looking south from Maesteg Castle Street Station. The Maesteg South signal box is in the foreground. In the background can be seen the goods shed which was the site of the first station at Maesteg, c.1963. (Courtesy John Morgans, Cymmer).

Nantyffyllon Station, c.1908. (Courtesy Miss Mair Jones, Nantyffyllon).

Railway staff on Troedyrhiw Garth Station, c.1900. (Courtesy Mr. B. J. Daniels, Cwmfelin, Maesteg).

Troedyrhiw Garth Station, c.1940. (Courtesy Mr. B. J. Daniels, Cwmfelin, Maesteg).

Cymmer General Station, 1954. (Courtesy J. Burrell, Bristol. Photograph by Graham Lloyd).

Looking north on the P.T.R. line at Talagwyn, approximately half a mile from the terminus at Pontyrhyll. Below the P.T.R. can be seen the G.W.R. to Bridgend. Map ref. 912886. Date 1908. (Courtesy Mrs. F. A. Morgans, Talagwyn).

64

The railway buildings of the disused Lletty Brongu Station, on the P.T.R. line, August 1977. (Courtesy Byron Gage, Dyffryn Rhondda).

Lletty Brongu Station sidings, 1949. (Courtesy John Morgans, Maesteg).

Cwmdu Station (P.T.R.) S.L.S. Special, May 1959. (The Real Photographs Collection, copyright Ian Allan Ltd.).

Maesteg Neath Road Station, 1954. (Courtesy J. Burrell, Bristol). Photograph by Graham Lloyd.

Maesteg Neath Road Station (P.T.R.) c.1910. The goods shed in the background was very similar to the one at Lletty Brongu Station. (Courtesy R. L. Pittard, Penyfai).

The Pontrhydycyff Viaduct, built in c.1897 to carry the P.T.R. over the Darran Valley.

Caerau Railway Bridge, demolished August 1981. In the foreground, on the right, is seen the Station Hotel. (Courtesy Lyn Phillips, Maesteg).

73

Engine No. 4144, 2-6-2T, leaving Llangynwyd Station for Bridgend, November 1962. (Courtesy R. M. Davies, Caerau).

A mineral train on the P.T.R. line after passing through Bryn Station. c.1960. (Photograph J. Morgans, Cymmer).

One of the two "Yankee" Engines, 0-8-2T, No. 21, that worked the P.T.R. line from Duffryn Yard to Pontyrhyll, c.1916. (Courtesy John Lyons, Maesteg).

"Yankee" Engine 0-8-2T, No. 21, on the P.T.R. line west of Cwmcerwyn Tunnel, c.1916. (Courtesy John Lyons, Maesteg).

An 0-6-2T G.W.R. Engine, No. 6676, crossing Caerau Railway Bridge. Date unknown. (Courtesy R. M. Davies, Caerau).

An 0-6-0PT leaving Caerau Tunnel, c.1957. (Courtesy R. M. Davies, Caerau).

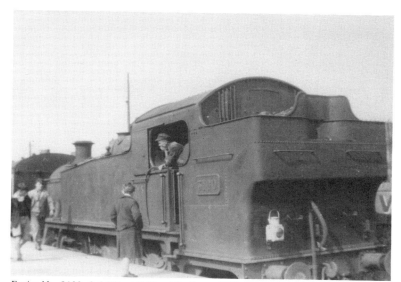

Engine No. 3100, 2-6-2T, at Bridgend Station, c.1950. (Courtesy R. M. Davies, Caerau).

2-6-2 No. 4121. Abergwynfi train, after arriving at Bridgend Station, June 1962. (Courtesy R. M. Davies, Caerau).

Passenger train on its journey to Maesteg Castle Street Station, after Troedyrhiw Garth Station. c.1930. In the background is the Garth Colliery.

LLYNVI AND OGMORE RAILWAY.

UP TRAINS.—WEEK DAYS.

FROM	a.m.		a.m.	p.m.	p.m.	p.m.	p.m.
Abergwynfi ......dep.	...	...	9 55	1 35		4 0	..
CYMMER	...	...	10 6	1 45		4 10	..
Tywith	...	...	10 13	1 55		4 17	..
MAESTEG ......dep.	7 15	...	10 21	2 3		4 25	4 25
Troedrhiew Garth...	7 19	...	10 25	2 7		4 29	6 29
Llangonoyd	7 23	...	10 29	2 11		4 33	6 33
Tondu Junction arr	8 5	...	10 35	...		4 30	6 40
Porthcawl ......dep.	...	9 45	10 0	..	Saturdays only. Market Train.	3 55	6 10
Pyle	...	9 5	10 13	..		4 9	6 21
Kenfig Hill	...		10 22	..		4 17	6 33
Tondu Junction arr	...		10 35	..		4 30	6 40
Nantymoel ......dep.	7 0	Via Pyle for Bridgend & up	10 5		1 20	4 5	6 10
Tynewydd	7 5		10 10	Saturdays only.	1 25	4 10	6 15
Hendreforglan	...		10 10		...	3 5	..
Black Mill	7 15		10 20		1 35	4 20	6 26
Brynmenin	7 23		10 27		1 43	4 2	6 33
Tondu Junction arr	7 25		10 30		1 46	4 3	6 36
Tondu Junction dep	7 35		10 41	2 23	1 50	4 4	6 45
BRIDGEND ...arr.	7 43	9 10	10 46	2 31	1 58	4 4	6 53

DOWN TRAINS.—WEEK DAYS.

FROM	a.m.	p.m.	p.m.	p.m.	p.m.	p.m.	p.m.	p.m.
BRIDGEND ... dep.	9 0	12 24	3 10	5 20	5 35	7 20	7 30	
Tondu Junction arr	9 9	12 35	3 9	5 29	5 37	7 29	7 37	
Tondu ....dep.	9 15	12 45		5 36	5 35	7 35	7 45	
Brynmenin..........	9 18	12 48	Saturdays only. Market Train.	5 40	5 40	7 39	7 44	
Black Mill	9 35	12 56		5 48	5 47	7 48	7 51	
Hendreforglan	9 43	3 46		6 16	6 18			
Tynewydd	9 35	1 12		5 56	5 59	7 55	8 3	
Nantymoel ....arr.	9 40	1 17		6 1	6 1	8 0	8 8	
Tondu Junction dep	9 13	12 40		5 32		...		
Kenfig Hill	9 31	12 58		5 44				
Pyle	9 32	1 5		5 53			7 30	
Porthcawl ......arr.	9 42	1 15	++				7 40	
Tondu Junction dep	9 12	12 40	3 12	5 32			7 33	
Llangonoyd	9 20	12 48	3 20	5 40			7 40	Saturdays only Market Train.
Troedrhiew Garth...	9 24	12 52	3 26	5 44			7 44	
MAESTEG ..... arr.	9 30	12 57	3 32	5 46			7 50	
Tywith	9 33	1 2	3 37				7 55	
CYMMER	9 43	1 10	3 45				8 2	
Abergwynfi	9 50	1 19	3 58				8 10	

A Market Train will leave Bridgend for Nantymoel at 3.10 p.m on Saturdays only, arriving at Nantymoel at 3.59 p.m

Llynvi and Ogmore Railway Time-table, in use between 1886-1901. The names of the various stations as they were then called make very interesting reading today, although there is an obvious error with one of the times of arrival stated.

78

P O R T H C A W L.

A GRAND GOOD TEMPLARS'

DEMONSTRATION

WILL BE HELD AT

PORTHCAWL ON WHIT-MONDAY,

JUNE 10th, 1878.

Programme of Proceedings :—

1. Procession of Members in Regalia, leaving the Railway Station at 1 p.m., accompanied by Three Bands of Music.

2. Amusements on the Green till 4 p.m.

3. Public Meeting on the Green at 4 p.m., when Addresses will be delivered by the following Gentlemen, (Brothers of the Order), viz.: G. A. Edwards, Esq., G.W.C.T.; W. T. Raper, Esq., R.W.G.T.; Rev. T. A. Pryce, P.D.D.; G. P. Ivey, Esq., G.W.T.; and Rev. T. Cole, D.G.W.C.T.

To enliven the Meeting several pieces of Music will be rendered by the Amalgamated Good Templar Choir.

Refreshments can be had in the National School-room, on the Green, any time during the day, at reasonable charges.

☞ Special Trains will run from Maesteg, Nantymoel, Hendreforgan, Bridgend, and intermediate Stations, at Special Cheap Fares.—See Railway Bills.

By the annexed Table the Annual quantity of Coal shipped by the different Traders is shewn for the last ten years, and the number of Vessels freighted with Coal and Iron, and it will be seen that in *ten months* of the current year upwards of eleven thousand Tons of Coal have been brought down *more* than in any other *twelve months* since the Port and Road have been formed— a pretty safe prognostic of the stability of the undertaking

	Tons of Coal.	No. Vessels, Coal & Iron.
1842	 6831	 207
1833	 8608	 214
1134	 6501	 126
1835	 7062	 166
1836	.... 8466¼	 226
1837	.... 9267¼	 232
1838	.... 14032¾	 228
1839	 18772	 339
1840	.... 18288½	 288
1841	 10193	 213
10 Months 1842	.... 29266¾	 478
Total Tons of Coal	**137,296¾**	**2717 No. of Vessels.**

The very considerable increase of the Coal Trade being the effect of the following causes.—

1st. *The Shipment of Coal has been found more profitable than using it in the manufacture of Iron.*

2nd. *The Coal workings have become better opened, and consequently a much larger Quantity is brought to light.*

3rd. *The Quality has been more tested, and accordingly appreciated.*

4th. *The Port has become better known, and its safety and facilities ascertained by experience.*

Coal tonnages, Porthcawl, 1832-1842.

Selected Rates.

Comparative Rates upon Coal to Port Talbot, Cardiff, and Barry, for Shipment.

COLLIERIES.	WHERE SITUATED.	Port Talbot Rate.	Cardiff Rate.	Barry Rate.
		d.		
North's Navigation Collieries	Maesteg ...	7	1/4	1/2
Garth Merthyr...	,, ...	8	1/4	1/2
Maesteg Merthyr	,, ...	10	1/4	1 2
Llynvi Valley (Ol'er H. Thomas)	Llynvi Valley...	10	1 4	1 2
Braichycynmer	Garw Valley ...	10	1 4	1 2
Bettws Llantwit	,, ...	10	1 4	1/2
Garw Fechan	,, ...	10	1/4	1 2
Ffaldau	,, ...	10	1/4	1 2
Oriental Merthyr	,, ...	10	1 4	1/2
Darran	,, ...	10	1/4	1 2
Nanthir	,, ...	10	1/4	1 2
International	,, ..	10	1/4	1 2
Ocean Garw	,, ...	10	1/4	1 2

The railway rates for the carriage of coal from the collieries in the Maesteg and Garw districts to Port Talbot, Cardiff and Barry Docks in 1905.

Selected Rates.

Comparative Rates upon Pitwood from Port Talbot and from Cardiff.

COLLIERIES.	WHERE SITUATED.	Port Talbot Returned Colliery Waggons. 6 ton loads.		Cardiff Returned Colliery Waggons. 6 ton loads.	
		s.	d.	s.	d.
Dyffryn Rhondda	Bryn, Port Talbot R'ly	0	10	3	9
Bryn Navigation	,, ,, ...	0	10	3	9
North's Navigation Collieries	Maesteg ,, ..	1	2	2	9
Garth, Merthyr	,, ,, ...	1	2	2	8
Llest	Garw Valley, via Port Talbot Railway ...	1	3	2	7
Braichycymmer	,, ,, ...	1	3	2	7
Garw Fechan	,, ,, ...	1	3	2	7
Ffaldau	,, ,, ..	1	4	2	8
Oriental Merthyr	,, ,, ...	1	4	2	8
Darran	,, ,, ...	1	4	2	8
Nanthir	,, ,, ..	1	4	2	8
International	,, ,, ...	1	4	2	8
Ocean Garw	,, ,, ..	1	4	2	8
Llynvi Valley	Llynvi Valley, via Port Talbot Railway ...	1	8	2	7
Bryndu Colliery	Cefn	1	2	3	4

The railway rates for the carriage of pitwood from Port Talbot Docks to the collieries in the Maesteg and Garw districts in 1905.

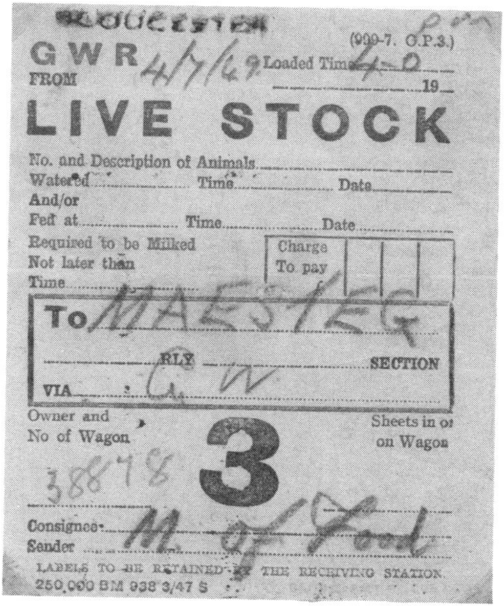

Wagon Labels.

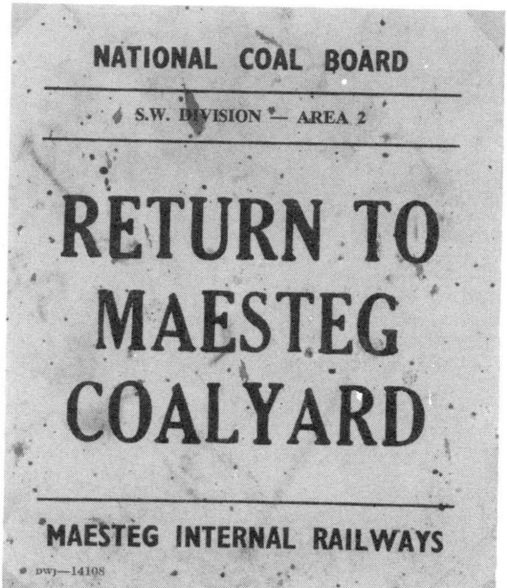

Runaway on the Cwmdu Colliery Mineral line, 1909.

"The last week of steam working from Tondu shed". An 0-6-0PT Engine, No. 4675, at Maesteg Castle Street Station, April 1964. (Courtesy Lyn Jones, Maesteg).

The last freight train on the former P.T.R. line, 2-8-0T Engine, No. 5213, 31st August, 1964. (Courtesy R. M. Davies, Caerau).

The last week of passenger traffic on the former G.W.R. Llynfi Branch line. Diesel crossing Caerau Bridge before entering Caerau Station. In the background can be seen empty coal trucks on the siding line connection from Caerau Colliery, June 1970. (Courtesy R. M. Davies, Caerau).

The last school train in the Llynfi Valley at Caerau Station, 14th July, 1970. (Courtesy R. M. Davies, Caerau).

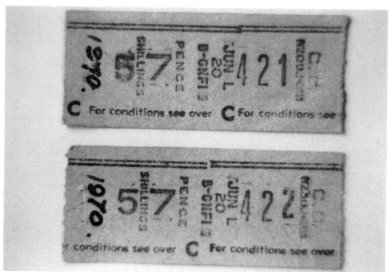

The last two passenger tickets purchased on the last train from Bridgend to Cymmer Afan Station on 20th June, 1970, this being the final day of passenger service on the line. (Courtesy Mrs. Glynis Hornby, Maesteg).

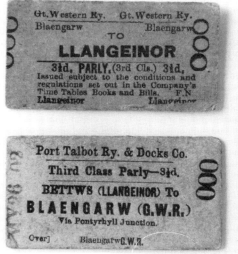

The above two passenger tickets were purchased on the same day, May 26th, 1902, it being the opening of the Blaengarw Station to passenger traffic. The journey to Blaengarw from Bettws Llangeinor was on the P.T.R. line, and the return journey was over the G.W.R. Garw branch line. (Courtesy Mr. and Mrs. Chilcott, Bettws).

Llynvi Junction, 2nd July, 1971. A visit from the Branch Line Society to view the preserved Engine Ex G.W.R. 0-6-0PT No. 9642. (Courtesy Lynn Jones, Maesteg).

A 3-car London suburban D.M.V. set approaching Llynvi Junction. Branch Line Society visit on 19th February, 1983. (Courtesy D. Maggs, Cymmer).

86

III. Collieries and the Maesteg
Internal Railway System

An early North's Navigation Company 0-4-0ST locomotive. (Courtesy W. Wells, Maesteg).

'Emma', 0-6-0ST. Stationary outside the old Maesteg Brewery, which was situated where the Coegnant Colliery Baths were lated sited. c.1910. (Courtesy W. Wells, Maesteg).

87

'Celia' 0-6-0ST. North's Navigation Railway, c.1910. (Courtesy W. Wells, Maesteg).

N.C.B. locomotive 'Maureen' leaving Caerau Colliery c. early 1970s. In the background can be seen Brewer's Bus Company's Garages. (Courtesy R. M. Davies, Caerau).

N.C.B. locomotive unnamed Bagnall 2766, leaving Maesteg Washery, early 1970s. (Courtesy R. M. Davies, Caerau).

N.C.B. locomotive, Bagnall 2766, backing up to Maesteg Washery, 1964. (Courtesy R. M. Davies, Caerau).

North's Navigation Railway locomotive 'Linda', approaching Maesteg Washery. (Courtesy Mr. Lynn Jones, Maesteg).

N.C.B. locomotive 'Maureen', on the occasion of the christening of the locomotive on 20th July, 1964. Sitting on the locomotive is Maureen, the daughter of Mr. J. Blackmore, the N.C.B. Group Area Engineer, and the driver, Mr. Cliff Wyn. (Courtesy Mr. Lynn Jones, Maesteg).

The former G.W.R. 0-6-0PT No. 9642, purchased for preservation by Lynn and Trefor Jones, Civic Week 1970. In the background can be seen the old engine shed and on the right can be seen the ruins of Nant-y-Crynwydd Farm house. (Courtesy R. M. Davies, Caerau).

The engine sheds on the site of the Old Llynvi Iron Works. (Date unknown). (Courtesy W. Wells, Maesteg).

91

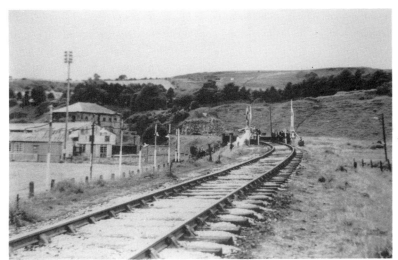

The old P.T.R. line skirting the Maesteg Rugby Football field. In the background is the old blast engine house of the Llynvi Iron Works. (Today it is incorporated into the buildings of the new Sports Centre). c.1971. (Courtesy Lynn Jones, Maesteg).

N.C.B. locomotive 'unnamed' Bagnall 2766, after a runaway on the steep inclined mineral line from St. John's Colliery, on the 12th May, 1971. The locomotive overran the stop block but fortunately no serious injuries occurred to the driver. Mr. Jim Blackmore is seen examining the locomotive, which incidentally was repaired at the Maesteg engine shed and put back into service within a few weeks. (Courtesy Lynn Jones, Maesteg).

Mr. Jim O'Flynn on the footplate of Ex-G.W.R. 0-6-0PT No. 9642. (owned by Lynn and Trevor Jones), which he often drove during public runs in the seventies. (Courtesy Mr. J. O'Flynn).

Caerau Colliery c. 1930's, with the Amy Johnson tip in the background. (Courtesy W. Hurd, Bryn).

93

St. John's Colliery, Maesteg, August 1983. (Courtesy John Lyons).

Coegnant Colliery, c.1980. (Courtesy Miss Sharon Goss, Nantyffyllon).

94

Garth Colliery, 1925. (Courtesy W. Hurd, Bryn). A mineral line connected the Garth Colliery to the G.W.R. Llynfi Branch, unlike the Oakwood Colliery which was situated directly alongside that line.

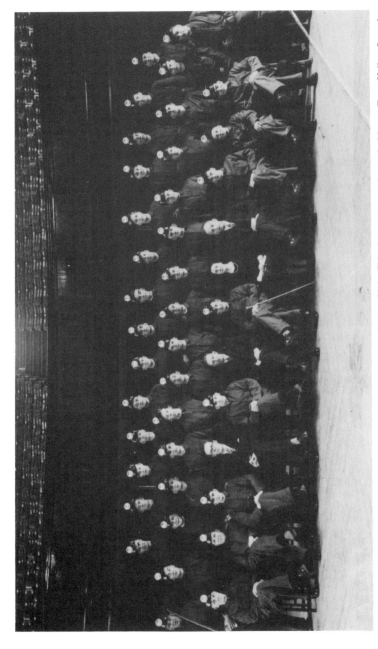

The Maesteg and District N.C.B. Choir, previously the North's Navigation Colliery Choir. This photograph was taken at the Maesteg Town Hall on September 14th, 1948, after a concert in aid of the 'Battle of Britain'. The conductor was Mr. S. H. Page, and the accompanist was Madam Dolly Powell Denford. The above choir also appeared at the Royal Albert Hall on 14th February, 1949. (Courtesy Wengof Rees, Nantyffyllon and I. James, Maesteg).

96

APPENDIX 1

Railway Preservation in the Llynfi Valley

To remind us of the type of engine used on the Llynfi Valley line, the brothers Lynn and Trevor Jones of Maesteg had an ex-G.W.R. pannier tank, engine number 9642, restored. It was housed at the old engine shed on the site of the Llynvi Iron Works until September 1975, after which time it was transferred to the new workshops at the Maesteg Washery. The engine was put into operation in 1970 as part of the Maesteg Civic Week celebrations. During the Seventies it was used for local excursions in the district in aid of charities. It may be mentioned that special excursions from railway societies such as the Monmouthshire Railway Society and the Branch Line Society came to Maesteg to view this preserved engine.

Footnote: Since April 1984 Engine No. 9642 has been under the guardianship of the 'South Wales Pannier Group'.

APPENDIX 2

Time Table Rules and Regulations – D.L. & P.R.

The Policeman and Weighers of the Company are to see that all Trains and Hauliers conform to this table, and are to keep the road clear for traffic at the times and places marked on the Table.

The Servants of the Company are authorised to remove from the line, on to a siding or convenient place all Trams and Trains obstructing the regular traffic; – all persons causing such obstructions or otherwise contravening this Table, will render themselves liable to Heavy Penalties provided in the Bye-Laws of the Company.

June 8th 1855   John Rhind – Superintendant

TIME TABLE.

LLYNVI VALLEY RAILWAY.

DOWN TRAINS.

TRAINS START FROM AND PASS	Miles.	A.M.	A.M.	A.M.		A.M.		P.M.	P.M.	P.M.
COEGNANT	16½			6 45		10 15		12 15	12 35	3 15
BOWRINGTON	16			7 0		10 30		12 30	1 10	30
MAESTEG	15			7 20		10 50		12 50	1 30	3 50
GARTH	14½			7 30		11 0		1 0	1 40	4 0
LLWYNDURIS	13½			7 50		11 20		1 20	2 0	4 20
TONDU	9½		7 25	9 25		P.M. 12 50		2 55	3 35	6 0
PARK	8		7 35	10 0		1 30		3 25	4 5	
FOES	7¼	6 0	8 10	10 15		1 45		3 40	4 20	
CEFN-CWSG	6	6 30	8 35	10 40		2 10		4 5	4 45	
BRYNDU	5½	6 45	8 45	10 50		2 20		4 15	4 55	
S.W. JUNCTION	5	7 0	8 55	11 0	P.M. 1 30	2 30		4 25	5 5	
TYDRAW	3¾	7 30	9 25	11 25	2 0	3 0		4 50	5 30	
CORNELLY	2½	8 0	9 45	12 0	2 30	3 30		5 15	6 0	
PORTHCAWL	0	9 0	10 45	P.M. 1 0	3 30	4 30		6 15		

UP TRAINS.

TRAINS START FROM AND PASS	Miles.	A.M.	A.M.	A.M.		A.M.	A.M.	P.M.	P.M.	P.M.
PORTHCAWL	0			6 0		9 45	10 45	12 20	1 25	3 30
CORNELLY	2½			7 15		11 0	12 0	1 35	2 40	4 15
TYDRAW	3¾			7 45		11 30		2 0	3 10	4 45
S.W. JUNCTION	5			8 15		12 0		2 30	3 40	5 15
BRYNDU	5½			8 45		P.M. 12 25		3 0	4 0	5 35
CEFN-CWSG	6			9 0		12 40		3 15	4 15	5 50
FOES	7¼			9 35		1 10		3 55	5 0	
PARK	8		8 0	10 0		1 30		4 15	5 25	
TONDU	9½	6 0	8 45	10 45		2 15		5 0	6 10	
LLWYNDURIS	13½	8 0	10 45	P.M. 12 45		4 15		7 0		
GARTH	14½	8 30	11 15	1 15		4 45				
MAESTEG	15	8 45	11 30	1 30		5 0				
BOWRINGTON	16	9 15	12 0	2 0		5 30				
COEGNANT	16½	9 40	12 25	2 25		5 55				

The POLICEMEN and WEIGHERS of the Company are to see that all Trains, Traders, and Hauliers, conform to this Table, and they are to keep the Road clear for traffic at the times and places marked in the Table.

The SERVANTS of the Company are authorized to remove from he line, on to a siding or convenient place, all Trams or Trains obstructing the regular traffic; and all persons causing such obstruction, or otherwise contravening this Table, will render themselves liable to the HEAVY PENALTIES provided in the Bye-Laws of the Company.

——— This denotes going into a parting.

June 8th, 18[illegible].

JOHN RHIND, Superintendent.

(Courtesy 'Paris House', Maesteg).

APPENDIX 4

The Locomotives of the Llynvi and Ogmore Railway

From July 1873 the Great Western Railway arranged to work the line and the locomotives were added to the Great Western stock at this time.

Locomotives in Stock as taken over by the G.W.R. in 1873

L & O No.	G.W.R. No.	Type	Maker	Date Built
1	919	O-6-OT	Sharp, Stewart	1865
2	920	,,	,, ,,	,,
3	921	,,	,, ,,	,,
4	922	,,	,, ,,	,,
5	923	,,	,, ,,	1869
6	915	2-4-O	R. Stephenson	1853 (a)
7	916	2-4-OT	,, ,,	1860 (a)
8	917	,,	,, ,,	,, (a)
9	918	,,	,, ,,	1855 (a)
10	924	O-6-OT	Black Hawthorn	1871
11	925	,,	,, ,,	1872
12	926	,,	,, ,,	1873

(a) West Cornwall locomotives received in 1868 in exchange for four broad gauge engines.

Most of these engines were withdrawn within a few years of the Great Western Railway taking over, and afterwards the line was worked by standard Great Western Railway engines.

APPENDIX 5

Port Talbot Railway

As from June 1908 P.T.R. locomotives were added to G.W.R. stock, but did not receive G.W. numbers until after the grouping on the 1st January 1922.

P.T.R. No.	G.W.R No.	Type	Maker	Date Built	With-drawn
3	815	O-6-OST	R. Stephenson	1897	1930
8	183	O-6-2T	,, ,,	,,	1929
9	184	,,	,, ,,	,,	1948
10	185	,,	,, ,,	,,	1929
11	186	,,	,, ,,	,,	1934
12	187	,,	,, ,,	,,	1935
13	188	,,	,, ,,	,,	1947
14	189	,,	,, ,,	1898	1930
15	816	O-6-OST	,, ,,	1897	1929
17	1358	O-8-2T	Sharp, Stewart	1901	1948
18	1359	,,	,, ,,	,,	1935
19	1360	,,	,, ,,	,,	1926
20	1378	,,	Cooke Loco	1899 (a)	1928
21	1379	,,	,, ,,	1899 (a)	1929
22	808	O-6-OST	Hudswell, Clarke	1900	1933
23	809	,,	,, ,,	,,	1928
24	811	,,	,, ,,	,,	1933
25	812	,,	,, ,,	,,	1934
26	813	,,	,, ,,	,,	1934
27	814	,,	,, ,,	,,	1930
36	1326	2-4-2T	Sharp, Stewart	1898 (b)	1930
37	1189	2-4-OT	,, ,,	1897 (b)	1926

(a) Built by Cooke Locomotive Co., Paterson, New Jersey, U.S.A.

(b) Purchased from Barry Railway, built 1890.

Note Some of the O-6-OSTs were used for dock shunting at Port Talbot and thus rarely worked on the section from Port Talbot (Central) to Pontyrhyll.

Steam Rail Motor

P.T.R. No.	Type	Maker	Built	Withdrawn
1	Steam Rail Motor	R.W. Hawthorn Leslie	1906	1920

Note The steam rail motor was used on passenger service between Port Talbot (Central) and Pontyrhyll from 1907 to 1915. In August 1915 it was sent from Duffryn to Swindon and put into store. Later, in 1920, after which time it was sold to the Port of London Authority and continued in use until 1926.

(E.R. Mountford, Caerphilly)

APPENDIX 6

*Instruction as to Working of Trains and Traffic on P.T.R.,
July 12th, 1913*
(Duffryn Line)

Down Trains, Dyffryn to Copper Works:- All down trains
proceeding towards Copper Works Box must be prepared to
come to a stand on the Bridge over the G.W.R. line and Vivian's
line.

Dyffryn Junction:- During the approach and passage of
Passenger Trains, Shunting must not be carried on in the
Sidings adjoining the Main lines, and the Signalman must not
lower the Signals until the shunting operations have ceased.

All Down Goods Trains working from Tanygroes to Aberavon
must have sufficient brakes pinned down to enable them to stop
at the Home signal or Signal Box for Aberavon junction, as may
be required.

Celluloid and Cwm Gwnea Sidings:- As far as possible, the
traffic to and from the Sidings must be worked by Pilot Engines
from Dyffryn. The Brakevan and a few Wagons of a Down
Train may be left standing on the Main Line whilst the engine
goes into the sidings to pick up, provided the Brakevan wheels
are chained and locked by padlock.

Tynyffram:- When Down Goods Trains are brought to a stand
at the Down Home Signal or in the Loop, the Guard in charge
must, before the Trains are re-started, pick up a few of the
brakes, so as to ease the 'pull' on the Train.

Bryn:- When Down Goods Trains are brought to a stand at Bryn
Down Home Signal the Guard in charge must, before the Trains
are re-started, pick up a few of the Brakes, so as to ease the 'pull'
on the Train.

The Brakevan of a Down Train picking up at Bryn may be left on
Main Line whilst the Engine goes into Colliery Siding, provided
the wheels are chained and locked with padlock.

The key of Colliery Gate to be taken back to the Signal Cabin.
During the day the porter will be responsible, and during the
night the Signalman.

West End of Tunnel:- All Down Goods Trains, after leaving
East End Signal Cabin must proceed cautiously into the tunnel,

and come to a stand at the mouth (West End) of the tunnel, to allow the Brakesman putting down sufficient brakes to ensure the trains being brought to a dead stand on the West End Loop, at which place the Guards must pin down brakes until the Drivers are satisfied there are sufficient down to enable them to have their trains thoroughly under control down the bank to Bryn and Dyffryn.

Two Brakesmen are stationed at West End of Tunnel, one from 8.00 a.m. to 6.00 p.m., and one from 6.00 p.m. to 4.00 a.m., to assist the Guards of Down Trains in putting down wagon Brakes.

Dyffryn Line
TOWN TRAINS
(Upon G.W. Line
Blaengarw to Pontyrhyll
Junction)

	Goods and Mineral.	Goods and Mineral.	PASS.	Pick up Goods and Mineral.	Goods and Mineral.	PASS.	Goods and Mineral.	Goods and Mineral.
	a.m.	a.m.	a.m.	a.m.	a.m.	a.m.	a.m.	p.m.

Blaengarw
Pontycymmer
Pontyrhyll
Pontyrhyll Sidings
Bettws (Llangeinor)
West Rhondda Siding
Lletty Brongu
Gellyhir
Garth
Cwmdu
North's Colliery Siding
Maesteg
East End of Tunnel
West End of Tunnel
Bryn
Tynyffram Loop
Celluloid Siding
Cwm Cyrnea Siding
Dyffryn Junction
Tanygroes Junction
Port Talbot & Aberavon (& S.B)
Port Talbot (Central)

A- No. 3 Down to cross No. 5 Up at West End.   H- No. 3 Down to cross No. 4 Up at Garth.   "Comm. J 12th 1913.

Dyffryn Line.
UP TRAINS
(Down on G.W. Line
Pontyrhyll Junction to
Blaengarw).

	Pick up Goods and Mineral (incl. Trpt.)	PASS.	Goods and Mineral.	PASS.	Goods and Mineral.	Passenger	Goods and Mineral.	Saturdays and Saturdays only. PASS.	Goods and Mineral.
	p.m.	p.m.	p.m.	p.m.	p.m.	p.m.	p.m.	p.m.	p.m.

Port Talbot (Central)
Port Talbot & Aberavon (& S.B)
Tanygroes Junction
Dyffryn Junction
Cwm Cyrnea Siding
Celluloid Siding
Tynyffram Loop
Bryn
West End of Tunnel
East End of Tunnel
Maesteg
North's Colliery Siding
Cwmdu
Garth
Gellyhir
Lletty Brongu
West Rhondda Siding
Bettws (Llangeinor)
Pontyrhyll Sidings
Pontyrhyll
Pontycymmer
Blaengarw

G- No. 9 Up to shunt at Tynyffram for No. 10 Up to pass, cross No. 8 Down at East End and cross 2.00 p.m. Passenger ex Blaengarw at Maesteg.

B- No. 14 Up to cross No. 13 Down at Maesteg.

D- No. 13 Up to cross No. 12 down at Bryn.

E- No. 12 Up to cross No. 11 Down at West End.

M- No. 11 Up to cross No. 8 Down at West End and cross at East End the 2.00 p.m. Passenger train from Blaengarw.

N- No. 15 up to cross No. 13 down at West End.

P- No. 10 Up to pass No. 9 up at Tynyffram.

"P.C." Comm. 12th 1913

G78

LLYNVI AND OGMORE BRANCHES

(Ogmore Branch Service discontinued)

WEEKDAYS

N—Passenger Trains cannot cross.

DOWN

	Double Line			Single Line				Crossing Stations	Train Token Stations
	From	To		From	To	Worked by			
LLYNVI BRANCH									
Bridgend	—	Tondu North		Tondu North	Maesteg South	Electric Train Token		Gelli Las Llangynwyd	Tondu North, Gelli Las, Llangynwyd, Maesteg South
Maesteg South	—	Caerau		Caerau	Abergwynfi	Electric Train Token		Cymmer N.	Caerau, Cymmer, Abergwynfi
OGMORE BRANCH									
Tondu	—	Brynmenyn Jn.		Brynmenyn Junction	Caedu	Electric Train Token		Blackmill N.	Brynmenyn Junction, Blackmill, Caedu
Caedu	—	Ogmore Vale North		Ogmore Vale North	Nantymoel	Electric Train Token		—	Ogmore Vale North, Wyndham Pits South, Nantymoel

Working Time Table of Passenger Trains on Llynvi and Ogmore branches for 9th June to 14th September inclusive, 1958.

106

G80

OGMORE AND LLYNVI BRANCHES
(Ogmore Branch Service Discontinued)

WEEKDAYS

UP

Station		
NANTYMOEL	dep	
Wyndham Halt	arr	41 F
	dep	41 F
Ogmore Vale	dep	
BLACKMILL	arr	77 F
	dep	
BRYNMENYN	arr	78 F
JN.	dep	
ABERGWYNFI	dep	32 F
Cymmer Afan	arr	44 F
Caerau	dep	226 R
Nantyffyllon	arr	49 R
MAESTEG	dep	50 F
Troedyrhiew Garth	arr	50 F
Llangynwyd	dep	95 F
TONDU	arr	—
BRIDGEND	dep	138 F
ABERGWYNFI	dep	
Cymmer Afan	arr	
Caerau	dep	
Nantyffyllon	arr	
MAESTEG	dep	
Troedyrhiew Garth	arr	
Llangynwyd	dep	
TONDU	arr	3146
BRIDGEND	dep	3115
	arr	3121

Working Time Table of Passenger Trains on Llynvi and Ogmore branches for 9th June to 14th September inclusive, 1958.

107

Appendix 9

NEW DIESEL TRAIN SERVICE
(Replacing existing Table 134)

3rd December, 1962 until 5th January, 1963.

BRIDGEND, CYMMER AFAN & TREHERBERT

WEEKDAYS ONLY — SECOND CLASS ONLY

		a.m.	a.m.	a.m.	a.m.	noon S	noon E	p.m.	p.m.	p.m.	p.m. S
Swansea (High St.)	dep.	—	7 55	8 30	10 30	12 0	12 0	3 10	4 45	7 25	9 10
Cardiff (General)	dep.	5 45	8 0	—	10 0	1p 0	1p 0	2 55	5 30	7A50	10 0
Bridgend	dep.	6 45	8 47	9 25	11 25	1p35	1p35	4 7	6 15	8 30	10 40
Tondu		6 52	8 54	9 32	11 32	1 42	1 42	4 14	6 22	8 37	10 47
Llangynwyd		6 59	9 1	9 39	11 39	1 49	1 49	4 23	6 29	8 44	10 54
Troedyrhiew Garth		7 2	9 4	9 42	11 42	1 52	1 52	4 26	6 32	8 47	10 57
Maesteg (Castle St.)		7 2	9 12	9 47	11 47	1 57	1 57	4 33	6 42	8 52	11 2
Nantyffyllon		7 12	9 3	9 52	11 52	2 2	2 2	4 38	6 47	8 57	11 7
Caerau		7 18	9 24	9 58	11 58	2 8	2 8	4 44	6 53	9 3	11 13
Cymmer Afan		7 21	9 26	10 1	12 1	2 11	2a11	4 48	6 56	9 6	11 16
Blaengwynfi	See Note	—	9 31	10 6	12 6	2 16	3 9	4 53	7 1	9 11	—
Blaenrhondda	D	—	9 40	10 15	12 15	2 25	3 18	5 2	7 10	9 20	—
Treherbert	arr.	—	9 43	10 18	12 18	2 28	3 21	5 5	7 13	9 23	—
Porth	arr.	—	10 51	10 51	12 51	2 51	3 51	5 51	7 51	9 51	—
Pontypridd	arr.	—	11 1	11 1	1 1	3 1	4 1	6 1	8 1	10 1	—

		a.m.	a.m.	a.m.	a.m.	a.m.	p.m.	p.m.	p.m. E	p.m. S	p.m.
Pontypridd	dep.	—	—	6 36	9 36	11 36	1 36	4 36	6 36	6 36	7 36
Porth	dep.	—	—	6 47	9 47	11 47	1 47	4 47	6 47	6 47	7 47
Treherbert	dep.	—	—	7 50	10 25	12p30	2 45	5 15	7 15	7 20	8 36
Blaenrhondda	See Note	—	—	7 53	10 28	12 33	2 48	5 18	7 18	7 23	8 39
Blaengwynfi	D	—	—	8 2	10 37	12 42	2 57	5 27	7 27	7 32	8 42
Cymmer Afan		6 40	7 45	8 52	10 42	12 47	3 3	5 33	7 33	7 38	8 47
Caerau		6 44	7 48	8 27	10 46	12 51	3 7	5 37	7 37	7 42	8 52
Nantyffyllon		6 49	7 51	8 53	10 53	12 55	3 11	5 41	7 41	7 46	8 56
Maesteg (Castle St.)		6 21	7 55	8 32	10 54	12 59	3 15	5 48	7 48	7 53	9 0
Troedyrhiew Garth		6 24	7 58	8 42	10 58	1 3	3 19	5 52	7 52	7 57	9 4
Llangynwyd		6 27	8 1	8 46	11 1	1 6	3 22	5 55	7 55	8 0	9 7
Tondu		6 34	8 8	8 53	11 8	1 13	3 29	6 2	8 2	8 7	9 14
Bridgend	arr.	6 40	8 14	9 0	11 14	1 19	3 35	6 8	8 8	8 13	9 20
Cardiff (Gen.)	arr.	7 40	8 50	9 52	11 52	2C52	4 35	6 52	9 0	9 0	10 32
Swansea (High St.)	arr.	8 27	9 26	10 9	12 35	2 25	4 59	7B35	9 10	9 55	10 40

A—On Saturdays dep. 7.15 p.m.

B—On 17th December, 1962 to 12th January, 1963 inclusive, and commencing 1st April, 1963, arr. 7.21 p.m.

C—On Saturdays, arr. 2.35 p.m.

D—Replaces service in Table 142 of W.R. Timetable.

S—Saturdays only.

E—Saturdays excepted.

a—arrival time. Departs for Treherbert at 3.4 p.m.

b—arrive 8.7 a.m.

p—p.m.

108

SPECIAL CHEAP RETURN FARES

At the same time as the introduction of the new diesel services between Bridgend and Treherbert, the following attractive cheap excursion fares are being introduced.

They are available by any train on the day of issue.

Commencing Monday, 3rd December, 1962.

TO	From Treherbert	From Blaenrhondda	From Blaengwynfi	From Cymmer Afan	From Caerau	From Nantyffyllon	From Maesteg	From Troedyrhiew Garth	From Llangynwyd	From Tondu	From Bridgend
	s. d.	s. d.	s. d.	s. d.	s. d.	s. d.	s. d.	s. d.	s. d.	s. d.	s. d.
Bridgend	4 0	3 3	3 9	3 3	3 3	2 9	2 9	2 9	1 6	1 0	—
Tondu	3 6	3 0	3 6	3 0	3 0	2 6	2 3	2 0	0 6	—	1 0
Llangynwyd	2 6	2 3	3 0	2 6	2 0	1 9	1 9	1 3	—	0 6	1 6
Troedyrhiew Garth	2 6	2 3	3 0	2 3	1 9	1 6	0 6	—	1 3	2 0	2 9
Maesteg	2 3	2 0	2 6	2 0	1 0	0 6	—	0 6	1 9	2 3	2 9
Nantyffyllon	2 0	1 9	2 3	1 9	0 6	—	0 6	1 6	1 9	2 6	2 9
Caerau	2 9	2 6	2 9	2 6	—	0 6	1 0	1 9	2 0	3 0	3 3
Cymmer Afan	1 9	1 9	0 6	—	2 6	1 9	2 0	2 3	2 6	3 0	3 3
Blaengwynfi	1 0	1 3	—	0 6	2 9	2 3	2 6	3 0	3 0	3 6	3 9
Blaenrhondda	0 3	—	1 3	1 9	2 6	1 9	2 0	2 3	2 3	3 0	3 3
Treherbert	—	0 3	1 0	1 9	2 9	2 0	2 3	2 6	2 6	3 6	4 0
Treorchy	—	—	—	—	3 9	3 6	3 9	3 9	3 9	4 0	4 3
Ystrad Rhondda	—	—	—	—	4 0	3 9	4 0	4 0	4 0	4 3	4 6
Llwynypia	—	—	—	—	4 3	4 0	4 3	4 3	4 3	4 6	4 9
Tonypandy & T.	—	—	—	—	4 3	4 3	4 3	4 3	4 6	4 6	4 9
Dinas Rhondda	—	—	—	—	4 6	4 3	4 6	4 6	4 6	4 6	4 9
Porth	—	—	—	—	4 9	4 6	4 9	4 9	4 9	4 9	5 0
Trehafod	—	—	—	—	5 0	4 9	5 0	5 0	5 0	5 3	5 3
Pontypridd	—	—	—	—	5 3	5 3	5 3	5 6	5 6	5 6	5 9

Appendix 10(a)

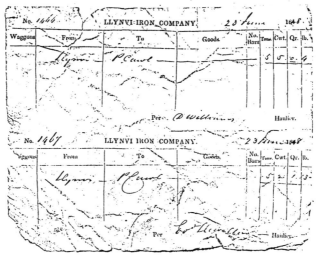

(Courtesy Mr. John Lyons, Maesteg).

Appendix 10(b)

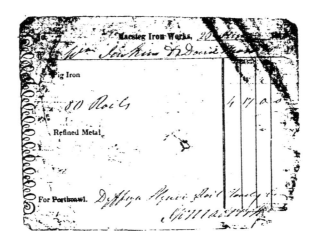

This Waybill, dated 20th June, 1845, was found in the beams of the roof at No. 1 Station Road, Llangynwyd, during building renovations. This building was previously the Llwyndyrys Weigh House. (Courtesy Mr. J. King).

Appendix 11

CHAPTER clxxvii.

An Act for authorising the Llynvi and Ogmore Railway Com- A.D. 1873.
pany to make new railways ; to deviate portions of existing
railways ; to raise additional capital ; to authorise arrange-
ments with the Great Western Railway Company ; and for
other purposes. [21st July 1873.]

WHEREAS it is expedient that the Llynvi and Ogmore Railway
Company (herein-after called "the Company") should be em-
powered to construct the additional railways and works, and to stop
up, divert, and alter respectively the roads and footpath in this Act
mentioned, and to take and hold for the purposes of the works by
this Act authorised, and for the general purposes of their undertaking, the lands and buildings in this Act also mentioned, and to
abandon and dispose of the portions of railway in this Act
mentioned :

And whereas plans of the intended railways and works, and of
the lands which may be taken for the same, and of the lands
which may be taken for other the purposes of this Act, and sections
of such railways, and a book of reference to such plans containing
the names of the owners or reputed owners, lessees or reputed
lessees, and occupiers of such lands, were deposited with the clerk
of the peace for the county of Glamorgan on or before the thirtieth
day of November one thousand eight hundred and seventy-two,
and are herein-after respectively referred to as the deposited plans,
sections, and book of reference :

And whereas it is also expedient that for the purposes of this
Act the Company be authorised to raise additional capital and to
borrow further sums on mortgage :

And whereas an agreement, bearing date the sixteenth day of
May one thousand eight hundred and seventy-three, has been
entered into between the Company and the Great Western Railway
Company with respect to the working by the latter company of the
railways of the Company and other matters ; and it is expedient
that the said agreement should be sanctioned and confirmed :

[*Local.—177.*] A 1

AN AGREEMENT between the Llynvi and Ogmore Railway Company (herein-after referred to as "the Llynvi Company") and the Great Western Railway Company (herein-after referred to as "the Great Western Company"), for the working and management of the railways, harbour, and works of the Llynvi Company by the Great Western Company, and for the division or apportionment of the tolls, rates, and charges to be taken upon the traffic herein-after referred to.

WHEREAS the Llynvi Company are owners of railways in the county of Glamorgan, extending from Porthcawl to Maesteg, and several other places, and they are also owners of a harbour and dock at Porthcawl already constructed, and are authorised to make and maintain other railways, some of which are in course of construction, and they have deposited a Bill in the Private Bill Office of the House of Commons for promotion in Parliament in the ensuing session for an Act to authorise the construction of other railways and to divert parts of their constructed railways, and to acquire lands for further station, siding, and other accommodation, and for other purposes, and to raise further capital for all or some of such purposes, and they are possessed of rolling stock, plant, stores, and materials :

And whereas the Great Western Company are the owners of a system of railways extending from Paddington to Milford Haven, which pass through South Wales, and they are also lessees for a long unexpired term of the Ely Valley Railway :

And whereas the railways of the Llynvi Company communicate with the railway of the Great Western Company at Bridgend, and also communicate with the Ely Valley Railway, and large quantities of traffic pass to and from the railways of the Llynvi Company and those of the Great Western Company, and it would be to the advantage of the public and to the interests of the Companies parties hereto if the railways, dock, and works, and the sidings, stations, locks, wharves, cranes, staiths, and other conveniences connected with the said railways and dock of the Llynvi Company (which railways and dock, and the sidings and other works and conveniences as aforesaid, and any other railways and works which the Llynvi Company may hereafter with the consent of the Great Western Company acquire or be authorised to construct, are herein-after called the undertaking of the Llynvi Company) were worked, maintained, and managed by the Great Western Company.

Appendix 12

G.W.R. Signal Boxes on the Port Talbot Railway

NAME AND PREFIX		OPENED	CLOSED
COPPER WORKS JUNCTION	1	1914	1949
	2	1949	5.2.1967
DUFFRYN NO. 3			31.8.1964
DUFFRYN NO. 1		1897	31.8.1964
DUFFRYN NO. 2	1	1897	1900
	2	1900	31.8.1964
TYN-Y-FFRAM		by 1912	31.8.1964
BRYN		1897	10.9.1964
WEST END TUNNEL LOOP	1	1900	c. 1912
	2	1911	31.5.1939
EAST END TUNNEL LOOP		1897	11.9.1934
MAESTEG (NEATH ROAD)		1897	31.8.1964
NORTH'S COLLIERY		1910	10.9.1964
CWMDU		19.11.1911	10.9.1964
GARTH		c. 1911	
LLETTY BRONGU		1897	c. 1911

(By kind permission of the Signalling Record Society).

NAME AND PREFIX		OPENED	CLOSED
BRIDGEND LLYNFI SIDING		1881	c. 1899
COITY JUNCTION	CS	c. 1900	30.11.1977
TONDU SOUTH		1901	26.5.1963
BROGDENS SIDING		1886	1901
TONDU MIDDLE	1		by 1886
	2	by 1886	
TONDU NORTH	1	1886	1901
	2	1901	12.11.1967
GELLI LAS		10.1.1943	19.3.1978
BETTWS		by 1884	
LLANGONOYD SOUTH		1895	1909
LLANGONOYD		1909	17.5.1965
LLANGONOYD NORTH		1895	1909
TROEDYRHIW GARTH		by 1890	by 1905
OAKWOOD		by 1890	
MAESTEG SOUTH		1897	9.5.1971
MAESTEG STATION		by 1890	1897
MAESTEG NORTH		1897	9.5.1971
LLYNVI JUNCTION	1		by 1886
	2	by 1886	21.11.1973
NANTYFYLLON SOUTH		1890	19.7.1966
NANTYFYLLON NORTH		1886	1966
COEGNANT SIDINGS		1884	13.11.1964
CAERAU		1898	8.5.1971
CYMMER		1886	17.6.1960

(By kind permission of the Signalling Record Society).

114

SOURCES OF INFORMATION:

Printed Sources:

ADAMS, G.F. – The Maesteg Tunnel. *In* Transactions of the South Wales Institute of Engineers.

BARRIE, D.S.M. – Railways of the Bridgend District. *In* The Railway Magazine, July 1955.
– A Regional History of the Railways of Great Britain. Vol. 12: South Wales. David & Charles, 1980.

BEVAN, Thomas – Dissertation on the industrial development of the Llynfi, Ogmore and Garw valleys, with special reference to transport facilities in the area. Unpublished M.A. Thesis, University of Wales, Cardiff, 1928.

EVANS, A. Leslie – The story of Taibach and district. Alun Books, 1982.

EVANS, Frederick – Tir Iarll. Educational Publishing Co., Cardiff, 1912.

EVANS, Thomas – Agricultural and farm notes. *In* Maesteg and District Festival of Wales Souvenir Brochure, 1958.

FLINT, A.J. – The Duffryn Llynvi and Porthcawl Railway, 1828-1860. *In* Morgannwg, Vol. XIII, Transactions of the Glamorgan History Society, 1969.

COOKE, R.A. – Track Layout Diagrams: the Llynfi Valley. The Author, Oxford.

HIGGINS, Leonard S. – John Brogden and Sons. *In* Glamorgan Historian, Vol. 10. Stewart Williams, 1974.

HOSEGOOD, John – The Great Western Colliery: Avon Colliery, Blaengwynfi. *In* Afan Uchaf, Vol. IV, 1981.

HUMPHRYS, Dr. Graham – The Industrial History of Maesteg. *In* Maesteg Town Hall Centenary Souvenir Brochure, 1982.

JOHN, H. – The Iron Industry of Maesteg in the Nineteenth Century: an Outline. *In* The Journal of the South East Wales Archaeological Society, Vol. 2, No. 2, 1976.

JONES, William – The Rhondda and Swansea Bay Revisited. *In* The Railway World Magazine, March 1970.

KING DAVIES, A. – Local Government and Civic Affairs. *In* Maesteg Town Hall Centenary Souvenir Brochure, 1981.
– Railways of the Llynfi Valley. *In* Maesteg and District Festival of Wales Souvenir Brochure, 1958.

MacDERMOT, E.T. – The History of the Great Western Railway, Vol. 2, 1863-1921. LONDON, 1927. (Revised by C.R. Clinker, 1964).

PAGE, J. – Forgotten Railways of South Wales. David & Charles, 1979.

PRAUDIERE, E. de la – Port Talbot and its Progress. Port Talbot Docks and Railway Company, Cardiff, 1919.

RANDALL, H.J. – Bridgend: the Story of a Market Town. R.H. Johns, Newport, 1955.

RICHARDS, Brinley – History of the Llynfi Valley. D. Brown & Sons, Cowbridge, 1982.

RICHARDS, S. – The Llynvi and Ogmore Railway. The Author, Norwich, 1977.
– The Port Talbot Railway. The Author, Norwich, 1977.

SMITH, Clive R. – Bygone Railways of the Afan. Alun Books, 1982.

ORDNANCE SURVEY MAPS, 1876, 1900.

Newspapers:

CAMBRIAN, January 10th, 1829; October 29th, 1830; November 30th, 1832.

GLAMORGAN GAZETTE, September 29th, 1950: 'The plan of the Ogmore dock and railway.'
September 18th, 1964: 'For the old P.T.R. – it's the end of the line.'
July 1st, 1966: 'Mid-Glamorgan railways.'

SOUTH WALES ECHO – September 30th, 1964: 'Chartered train from Maesteg to Paddington.'

Personal Information:

Mrs. Anne Jones – Details of early road transport in the Maesteg area.

E.R. Mountford – Additional data applicable to the history of the Llynfi Valley railways.

J. O'Flynn – Notes on the Maesteg Internal Railway System.

R. Pittard – Notes on the G.W.R. Llynfi Branch.

Mrs. Lynne Self – Details of the coal industry in the Maesteg District.

Other Sources:

Valuation List for Llangynwyd Higher, 1891. Glamorgan County Record Office.

Tithe Map of Maesteg District, 1841. Glamorgan County Record Office.

Llynfi Valley Railway Map, 1859. Glamorgan County Record Office.

Plan of Proposed Railway from Aberafan to Blaen Caerau, 1864. Clive R. Smith.

Cwmdu Board of Health Minutes, 1858-75. Glamorgan County Record Office.

T.C. Evans (Cadrawd) Collection, 2330 MS 59. Cardiff Central Reference Library.